Dedication

For my parents and my siblings Desiree, Richard, and
never stopped believing . . .

Table of Contents

Introduction

"Getting a job in investment banking is far from easy, but there are concrete rules to follow that will make the difference between getting an offer or getting a disappointing rejection."

The Real World of Banking

Flying overnight to Europe for meetings, dealing with multi-billion dollar clients and making six figures a year sounds like a glamorous life. Many undergraduates majoring in finance, business or accounting seek this lifestyle post-graduation. But what some undergraduates don't take into consideration when they choose their future career in investment banking is the exhausting dedication and hard-work the industry demands.

Before I discuss the steps you need to take, I'll describe my path to investment banking. I went to college at Boston University, where I completed degrees in Finance and International Relations. At B.U., I was trained at the Career Office as a resume editor. After I graduated, I worked in J.P. Morgan's Mergers and Acquisitions Group. I spent four years in New York and executed a number of multi-billion dollar deals across industries, including the sale of The Weather Channel and www.weather.com, the sale of Goodyear's Engineered Products Division, and the merger of R.H. Donnelley and Dex Media, among many others.

I was fortunate to be ranked at the top of my investment banking class four years in a row. Despite the economic crisis and the firm's downsizing, I was promoted to Associate in 2008 and worked on complex projects like the government bailout of GM and Chrysler. I formally recruited at undergraduate and graduate institutions on behalf of J.P. Morgan during that time, so I know what banks look for when hiring candidates.

I have done speaking engagements at Harvard and Boston University on the subject of getting into investment banking at both the analyst and associate levels. Over nearly the past decade, I have coached dozens of individuals and successfully helped them get jobs in investment banking.

After working in Investment Banking, I completed my MBA at Harvard Business School, where I served as Career Representative for my class and advised students on their career search, resumes, cover letters, interviews, and offer negotiations.

Getting a job in investment banking is far from easy, but there are concrete rules to follow that will make the difference between getting an offer or getting a disappointing rejection. It is one of the most structured recruiting processes of any dream job, so following these simple rules can go a very long way!

Why Investment Banking?

"Banking is the boot camp of jobs. It's extremely challenging, takes a lot of hard work, long hours, and the exposure you earn working with top-level business leaders and corporations can definitely open the door to multiple careers outside of the bank."

Why Investment Banking?

Choosing the right career field is a lot like finding a perfect pair of pants: you need pants that feel comfortable, instill confidence, and provide plenty of years of wear. You don't want to pick a pair off the rack because they project a certain image—you may wear them a few times and find that you hate them. The same can be said of going into investment banking for all the wrong reasons.

Finding out what excites you about the industry is really important and can help you choose the right division of investment banking. Religiously reading current financial trends and news, like *The Wall Street Journal,* can help you identify what deals and business transactions you find the most riveting.

If you discover that you're fascinated with asset management deals or investing in the markets, investment banking may not be your cup of tea. Those are different divisions of a bank that deal with investments and personal finance. On the other hand, if you find you're following mergers or if you're interested in why this company just decided to go public, then investment banking is for you. If you find that you are on the fence between investment banking and another division of a bank, taking a look at some of the reasons to go into the field, or not, may prove helpful in your decision.

Before my senior year of college, I interned at Citigroup Asset Management in London. While I enjoyed the internship and learning more about securities (in my case, mutual funds), I realized that I liked being more on the inside of a company rather than just evaluating it from the outside as a finished product. I wanted to be a part of the making of this "product," i.e. the company. Asset managers decide what companies to invest in that will maximize returns for their clients, but investment bankers help to shape those companies.

I wanted to contribute to how those companies evolve and witness how C-suite executives and boards tackle big company decisions. One natural career path would have been to work in the strategy group of a major company, but I was not ready to commit to one firm in one industry at this early stage in my career. I realized that banking would expose me to numerous Fortune 500 companies and how they think, rather than give me a lot of exposure into only one of those firms.

It was important to evaluate the types of decisions I would learn about; in banking, they would specifically be decisions dealing with accessing capital (e.g. debt, equity, IPO, etc.), selling part of or the entire company, and growing through mergers, acquisitions, joint ventures and other types of structural changes. I would not get to work on growing the company organically, which is accomplished primarily through product development (e.g. Should we add a watermelon flavor to our sorbets? What features should we include in the next generation iPad?) and business development (e.g. How can we sell more to our top customers? How can we reach new customers in Lebanon?).

The other reason I chose investment banking is because of the fast-paced environment; it appealed to my personality. I liked the idea of starting my career in a job that would put me right in the fire of things! During my internship at Citi, I visited various groups throughout the bank during my free time. I felt that the culture in the banking division was the best fit for me, despite the long hours and stressful workload. I knew I was ready to work hard in whatever business job I chose after graduation, and I wanted that hard work to go towards something that would make a big impact.

Question:

I recently finished reading your book and found it extremely useful in terms of the information it offered and the insight it had on what it was like to work in investment banking. Now I feel as though I have a much stronger grasp as to what investment banking is and how to get into it.

However, I am still unsure if it is the career path for me and I would actually like to know more about your asset management internship with Citigroup; can you help compare the two experiences?

Answer:

I'm glad you found the book useful. Asset Management is a great career path; it just differs from banking in a number of ways:

1. *The most important is that you will learn to look at the market as an outsider vs. an insider.*

   - *In Asset Management, you will learn to study market dynamics, why stocks/bond/securities go up or down based on economic data, company data, political events, etc. Your "clients" will be investors.*

   - *In banking, your clients will be companies and you won't study the market much except when you are considering timing to announce a deal, the impact of a deal announcement on a company's stock, and the market's perception of value. You will instead work on shaping the company from the inside and help it execute on the vision it hopes to deliver to shareholders. As you can see, your responsibilities as an employee are already very different. In one case, you will learn to invest and in the other, you will learn to advise and create.*

2. *Your schedule in Asset Management follows the market more, so you start early and end in the evening. Hours are more structured and predictable. In banking, you start later but there is no deadline for when you go home, so your hours tend to be a bit longer.*

3. *Asset Management is somewhat less stressful and less fast-paced than banking, but still extremely stimulating, especially if you focus on a great product or work under the supervision of an interesting portfolio manager. Banking can be more stimulating for those who thrive on the thrill of getting "deals" done rather than working on ongoing assignments.*

The best way to determine which path is for you is to speak to people who work in these two divisions, ask specific questions pertinent to your skills and what motivates you, and try to either shadow them for a few hours or intern.

Job Shadowing Opportunities

When considering a career in investment banking, you should start talking to people in the industry very early on in your undergraduate career. If you are out of college, and are considering switching into banking from a career like consulting, networking with industry bankers is even more important.

You may even try "shadowing" bankers at work one day by joining them at their desks and gaining an insider's look at what they do on a daily basis: it's one of the best ways to know if you can survive and thrive in the fast-paced work environment. When I was an undergraduate, I didn't even know this was possible! But I've had many interested candidates over the years reach out to ask if they could shadow me for a few hours.

Contacting an alumnus is the best way to schedule a job shadow. And keep in mind: it was always easier for me to say yes to a candidate when they made it clear that they would be careful to stay out of my way and not interfere with my workflow, which was often under tight deadlines. Saying something along these lines in your request helps the bankers feel more comfortable that you have the right expectations about the meeting; it will be a job shadowing visit, not a babysitting session.

I would always end up spending at least half an hour chatting with the candidate, answering questions about what I was working on, and explaining the various activities that I'm involved in during my days. Most bankers are happy to allow this as long as they can maintain the confidential nature of the projects they're working on (typically done by masking company names).

Additionally, some banks offer formal shadow days, especially to minorities and women, so it's worth contacting the H.R. offices or browsing the company website to see if you can participate in any programs. You can view the visit as a sort of mini-internship to help you determine if the job is right for you. All the info you gain will also help you better answer interview questions if you do decide to apply. As always, try to use every encounter to impress!

Question:

In terms of asking alumni if I can shadow them, is there a specific time of the

year or month that would increase my chances of getting favorable responses? Should I aim for a month like August when it is typically slower?

Answer:

August is by far the slowest month around the office but it's not necessarily the best for shadowing. You will likely see a little less action than usual, but you will definitely have a better chance at convincing a junior banker to meet with you since work is typically slower. There is no particular time of the year that is best, so you will have to be flexible. Bankers are always busy and can unexpectedly become tied up on assignments, so let them know that you understand the meeting time may change. If you plan on visiting from out of town, you should inform the banker so he or she is less apt to cancel altogether and can potentially have you shadow someone else who has more downtime. Also, try to plan your visit over more than one day in case your meeting gets rescheduled.

In general, Fridays are slowest because some senior members and clients may be out of town and Mondays are typically the busiest. Most junior team members have some downtime right after lunch and before the evening work begins, so offer to stop by in the afternoon rather than in the morning.

Make sure you start by building a solid relationship with any contacts or alumni. Begin with an informational meeting over the phone or ideally in person, and then work your way up to a shadowing session. Asking for a shadowing session as your first meeting may be asking too much.

Pros and Cons

3 Reasons to Choose Investment Banking

1. **High Learning Curve.**

Recent finance, business, or accounting college grads find that a career in investment banking offers one of the highest learning curves out there. Within your first year of banking you are exposed to top business leaders, how they think, how they create strategy for the Fortune 500 companies they manage, and the thought processes behind these decisions.

2. **Opens Doors to Other Careers.**

Banking is the boot camp of jobs. It's extremely challenging both mentally and physically, takes a lot of hard work, and the exposure you earn working with top-level business leaders and corporations can definitely lead to many careers outside of the bank. A job in banking stamps your career passport with, "hard-worker, contributor, proactive self-starter, and team player."

3. **Insiders Pass to a Life-Long Network.**

Once you're in, you're on the inside. Investment bankers are a group of smart and fun individuals. They like to live by the motto "Work hard, and play hard." They undoubtedly work tremendously hard, but once you work hard alongside them, you too become a member of the permanent network. I still keep in touch with quite a few of my former colleagues, many of whom have pursued various career paths after banking, and some who have risen through the ranks and will likely someday become Group Heads!

3 Reasons Not to Choose Investment Banking

1. **Glamour, Glitz, and Glory.**

It's 7 a.m., time to start your shift. This is after you went to bed at 3 a.m. following a 15 hour-plus day, and you can't see straight. Then, you get a phone call in the afternoon telling you to jump a flight to Germany because the associate on the deal can't make it. Most people think, "It's great! You get to go to Germany. That's exciting." Yes, you will travel business or first class, and maybe you're lucky and will sit next to someone interesting or important. But chances are you will barely get to speak to that person because you will either be expected to work throughout the flight, or you will look so much like a zombie that you'll rely on your eye mask to hide the exhaustion.

This is the life of an investment banker. No two days are alike, except the fact that you're working hard each day. Sometimes, for some miraculous reason, your deals are all quiet and you get offered a couple of tickets to that night's big game. In my first week on the job, I got front-row tickets to the U.S. Tennis Open and got to watch all my favorite players up close! Some days feel glamorous when you have access to some of the most powerful people in the world and get to meet a business leader you had studied in college. Otherwise, there is very little glory with a few hours of sleep during multiple days.

2. **You Make a Ton of Money.**

It's a well-known myth that investment bankers are rolling in dough. Well, let's back up a little. There is some truth to the myth. The field does pay on the high side, when you consider that you're coming out of undergrad or grad school. You most likely make more than any of your friends. But when you do the math and you take your first year's salary (which is the only guaranteed portion of your compensation) and divide it by the number of hours worked, it's a little more than minimum wage.

You put in around 100 hours a week, and weekends start to blend into weekdays, nights are days, and holidays come and you think, "Wait. Is it really Christmas this week?! I haven't bought a single gift!" Of course, on the flip side, most minimum wage jobs wouldn't let you work a lot more than 40 hours a week, so maybe it is a lot more money than a lower wage job. Now, finding the time to spend the money you make—that's another story.

3. **"I Am . . .**

Hard-working . . . Better equipped at working in the fast-lane . . . Dedicated to my work, no matter how many hours I have to put in." While these are great qualities to have to get into the field, nothing can really prepare you for the amount of work that happens in banking and the toll it takes on you—emotionally, physically, and mentally.

Students always ask me if the hours really are as bad as people say they are. The short answer is largely "yes." Even the hard work and little sleep that come from writing a paper and preparing for 2 back-to-back midterms in college can't prepare you for a 16 straight hour work day, where one wrong number can cost a client millions of dollars—

nothing will really equate to that level of stress. The effect it has on your body and mind are probably incomparable to what you have experienced up until that point in your life.

Of course there are ways to alleviate them, like getting more efficient at your work (the first year is the hardest!), selecting certain groups, and having the right support from friends and family. I was working on a joint venture during my first year as an analyst (they are so hard to execute!) and had a few days in a row when I would come back to my midtown Manhattan apartment around 5 a.m. or later, with just enough time for a quick nap and a shower before heading back to the office.

One morning when I came home the sun was already up, and I found a magazine from my roommate Lauren cut up and laying neatly on my bed. It read: "All-nighters are for clubs, not cubicles." Ironically, it was an ad for an energy drink, which I certainly felt like I needed! It made me smile and I later hung it in my cubicle as a reminder to take nights off. Having the support of a close friend or roommate (preferably someone who is also a banker like mine!) is the key to making it through the long hours—and maybe even enjoying them.

III.

Understanding Investment Banks

"Bankers strategize with CEOs and executive teams about where the company is headed. The public might hear the outcomes of those strategy sessions . . . but they don't get the insider's scoop that goes into that thinking process."

Breaking Down The Basics

Investment banks act as the intermediary between sources of capital and uses of capital —those who have capital and those who need it. Sources of capital come from various places, such as retirement funds, people's deposits, and any cash that people don't need immediately which can be put to use. What those people want is a return on their investment.

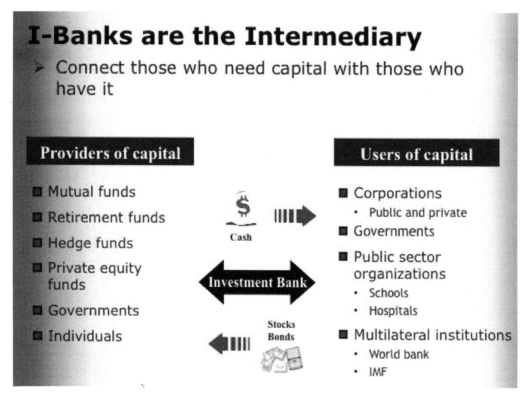

Investors essentially share their cash with companies, and the companies issue bonds and stocks as a promise of repayment and some return (e.g. interest or dividends). The investment banks help companies access this pool of cash to fund expansion projects, acquisitions, and all the things that companies need to thrive and grow.

Most banking opportunities are in major financial hubs like New York or London. Many banks also have regional offices in cities such as Chicago, San Francisco, Houston and Los Angeles, or abroad in Tokyo, Hong Kong, Sydney, Sau Paulo, or Paris. Getting recruited for these smaller regional offices is more difficult as there is a more limited number of spots.

But if investment banking truly is your calling, there is a job out there for you—yes, even after the economic crisis. The truth of the matter is that recruiting for banking has been consistent for the past 20 or 30 years. Since the downturn of the economy, there have been some tweaks in recruiting. To note: banks are pulling from their intern pool rather than aggressively recruiting from colleges as they have in the past.

Investment banks are assessing their recruiting tactics in a more refined manner and filling an entire group's need of around seven analysts directly from the summer's intern class. Banks are still searching for the best of the best, so if you can work extremely hard, follow the proper chain of command (which includes a high GPA, networking, extracurricular activities, etc.), and land yourself an internship, you are 99% on your way to a career in investment banking.

Of course, you're going to have to really, truly, without-a-doubt prove yourself worthy for that last 1%. And that starts with an understanding of the basics.

Investment Bank Divisions

Investment banks are typically divided into 3 main groups:

1. **Corporate Finance**

2. **Sales and Trading (S&T)**

3. **Equity Research**

When you hear people say they want to get into "investment banking," they're referring to the corporate finance component. Otherwise, they would say "I want to be a trader" (Sales and Trading), or "I want to do research" (Equity Research). Traders and researchers take public information from firms and feed it into their models in order to predict outcomes about the market.

Unlike traders and researchers, corporate finance investment bankers are privy to information that requires them to sign confidentiality agreements. They get an insider's look into the minds of companies and their projections beyond the next year, information not shared with the public and safeguarded for competitive reasons. Bankers strategize with CEOs and executive teams about where the company is headed. The public might hear the outcomes of those strategy sessions ("we are selling a division" or "we are issuing a bond to fund an expansion abroad"), but they don't get the insider's scoop that goes into that thinking process.

Investment bankers often help to build those projections for the next five to ten years based on a number of potential scenarios. When advising a client on the sale of their company, investment bankers will help to create long-term projections to provide to potential buyers. The buyers will need these to determine how much to bid for the company and how much it's worth to them. The process often involves working with huge messy spreadsheets and hundreds of small assumptions that the client uses to estimate their future revenues and profits. It can definitely get confusing, and may likely cause a little brain damage to get up to speed on models that took the client years to develop . . . but it's also fun!

If you like numbers and puzzles, you'll probably enjoy financial modeling. You'll spend many a night jamming to music on your headphones while trying to figure out how these client models work and how you can expand them to estimate longer-term projections. It's also a great learning experience to see how the top companies in the world think about managing their businesses (e.g. Do they estimate future performance by geography, customer type, or product? How do they set pricing? How do they manage costs?)

To ensure that there is no conflict of interest between bankers and the traders or researchers who are making investment decisions about the same clients, the two sides of a bank are divided by a figurative Chinese wall. Those who work on either side of the bank cannot contact the other side—not even via email. Otherwise, sharing client names or other pending deal info could lead to insider trading and other fraudulent activities. Most roommates in banking end up being on one side or the other to make things a bit simpler at home, so choose your roommates wisely!

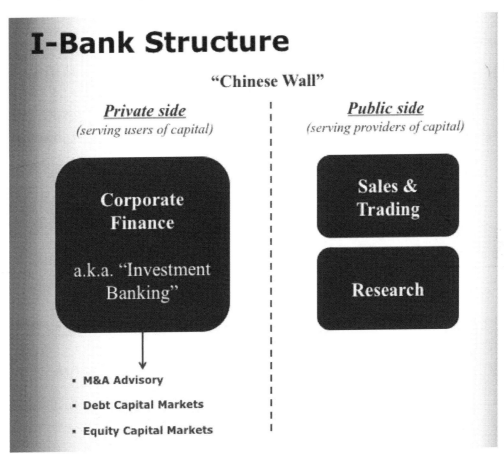

This regulation also prevents confidential information from falling into the hands of the public and helps explain why bankers work on deals long before they are formally "announced" to the market. If the public found out about them prematurely, they would start betting on those stocks and impact deals before those deals were fully negotiated.

Selecting an Investment Bank Division

When you are considering a career at an investment bank, ask yourself:

- What are my strengths?

- What do I love most about finance as an academic subject?

Based on your answers, you might be looking at a career as a trader in Sales and Trading (S&T), a researcher for Equity Research, or an analyst or associate for Corporate Finance (i.e. "Investment Banking"). Within each division of investment banking, there are multiple groups and products that you can choose from. This is where knowing what you're interested in and the things you are good at comes into play.

When I was making my decision, I started by asking myself whether I wanted to learn about investing in the markets (i.e. S&T or Equity Research) or whether I wanted to help companies evolve and make strategic decisions. I was always a lot more interested in getting into the minds of companies rather than maximizing return for investors. I read *The Wall Street Journal* daily and paid attention to what deals interested me. For me, it was always Mergers and Acquisitions (M&A) deals.

To be a trader, you have to be decisive and ready to take quick action. But at this early stage in my career, I was not excited by the idea of feeling the stress of erratic market dynamics. I wanted to work on projects that would take a long time to complete (months, not days or hours) so that I could solidify my business learning. I also liked the idea of working closely with clients and getting to know the management teams of those companies.

Keep in mind: once you decide which division you want to pursue within an investment bank, it is difficult to switch—so do your homework, and network as much as possible to make the right choice. Pay attention to what aspects of finance you find exciting and ask bankers what they like or dislike about their jobs to dig deeper.

Key Services & Your Role

Investment banking represents a multitude of services, including advising on Mergers and Acquisitions (M&A) and accessing capital to fund activities through the issuance of debt, equity, or by going public (an I**nitial Public Offering, IPO**). The banks provide advice to clients as well as helping them to execute on these transactions once they decide to move forward. Bankers work on deals that involve high-profile clients and get to watch the process that companies take to make these big decisions. Often, this involves listening to board meetings that involve some of the world's leading business minds.

I remember the first time I attended a Board meeting. It was during my first year as an analyst, and I was replacing the Associate on my team who had to travel abroad for another deal. The company was in the energy sector, which is regulated by the government to ensure that customers don't incur excessive prices on basic needs like electricity. The Board, made up of CEOs, professors, and various experts, was convened to approve or reject the sale of the company to a suitor in another state. The sizeable offer was ultimately rejected, but it was so interesting to hear the various considerations —like the potential impact on customers and the community.

When a deal is completed, it often involves a big event that changes the evolution of that company permanently and impacts all company stakeholders (e.g. shareholders, employees, customers, etc.). In investment banking, you will be privy to the behind-the-scenes, confidential meetings that put these plans into motion. You begin to realize that there are a number of reasons why a beverage company would want to acquire a chip company that operates in a seemingly different industry, like the benefit of sharing distribution channels and reaching the same customers. There is also the added perk that bankers often get the satisfaction of watching the fruits of their labor discussed in major publications like *The Wall Street Journal* and global television networks.

Some people are drawn to the investment banking field because they want to learn about issuing stocks or bonds. At what price should a stock be issued? For example: I know how much a shoe will cost me (it usually comes with a price tag!), but what about trying to figure out how much a piece of the entire shoe company would cost? That requires another level of analysis that bankers in the equity group will master. Even if you figure out how much the shoe company is worth, you still have to figure out how to convince investors of this, and how much to price the stock so that you get enough investors to buy in, while also ensuring that the client is getting properly compensated for the shares they sell.

Top Investment Banking Firms

Bulge bracket is the term used for the largest investment banks in the world. This includes the three firms known as the "superbanks" that offer all banking services:

- J.P. Morgan,

- Citigroup, and

- Bank of America Merrill Lynch.

The other bulge bracket investment banks are Morgan Stanley, Goldman Sachs, UBS, Credit Suisse, Deutsche, and, more recently, Barclays.

Smaller firms are called "boutiques" and tend to specialize in particular parts of the market such as in an industry, a product, or certain deal sizes. Examples of well-known and fairly large boutiques include Evercore Partners, Greenhill, Lazard , and Jefferies, among many others. The recruiting done at these firms is less structured and the overall experience differs from that of classic "investment banking", which is usually used to refer to bulge bracket firms.

Some banks are well-known experts in certain industries. The performance of top investment banks is tracked closely through the use of **league tables**. League tables help to keep track of the banks that are considered the best in each industry. These tables are published quarterly and annually to show the ranking of top banks through various metrics such as fees generated, number of deals completed, value of deals announced, etc. The two most respected sources for league tables in the industry are Dealogic and Thomson Reuters.

Though both of these sources restrict their league tables to members, anyone can view the year's most up-to-date league tables via the *Financial Times*. Below you'll find a preview of the 2011 league tables and some very preliminary tallies on how 2012 is shaping up (or simply go to www.ft.com/leaguetables):

Top 10 Banks	Fees ($m)	Change in Fees vs. Prev Period*	% of Fees collected by product in 2011			
			M&A	Equity	Bonds	Loans
JP Morgan	5,459.19	+1%	29	20	25	26
Bank of America Merrill Lynch	4,879.97	+8%	24	20	26	30
Morgan Stanley	4,040.08	-1%	42	28	21	10
Goldman Sachs	3,912.52	-10%	46	24	21	9
Credit Suisse	3,388.52	+1%	35	23	25	17
Deutsche Bank	3,164.56	-2%	28	23	33	16
Citi	3,120.19	0%	23	21	31	24
Barclays	2,750.65	+1%	27	20	32	21
UBS	2,345.67	-7%	45	26	21	9
Wells Fargo	1,599.14	+28%	9	17	24	50
Total	**79,827.31**	-1%	39	21	20	21

Quarterly trends by Product

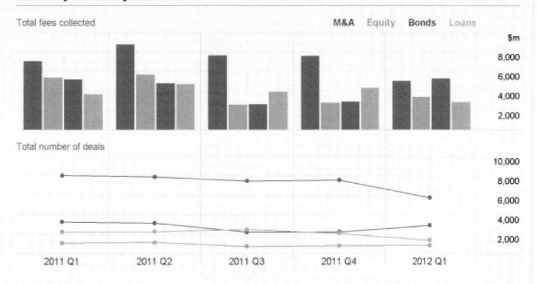

Total fees collected

M&A Equity **Bonds** Loans

$m

8,000
6,000
4,000
2,000

Total number of deals

10,000
8,000
6,000
4,000
2,000

2011 Q1   2011 Q2   2011 Q3   2011 Q4   2012 Q1

Data from Jan 1 2011 - Dec 31 2011 and Jan 1 2010 - Dec 31 2010
* No activity in comparable period

Data as of Mar 28 2012

 THOMSON REUTERS    Freeman Consulting Services

Banking leaders (based on fees)
A table of the most dominant investment banks; by products, regions and industries.

	Category	Bank	YTD 2012 Fees ($m)*
Products	Global Investment Banking	JP Morgan	1,260.48
	Bonds	JP Morgan	491.16
	Loans	JP Morgan	309.34
	Mergers & Acquisitions	Morgan Stanley	273.61
	Equity	JP Morgan	273.33
Regions	Americas	JP Morgan	948.67
	Europe	Deutsche Bank	309.05
	Japan	Sumitomo Mitsui Finl Grp	162.81
	Asia Pacific (ex Central Asia)	UBS	120.71
	Africa/Middle East/Central Asia	Morgan Stanley	14.29
Industries	Financials	JP Morgan	324.99
	Energy & Power	Credit Suisse	202.23
	High Technology	JP Morgan	144.40
	Materials	JP Morgan	136.88
	Industrials	Deutsche Bank	127.96
	Real Estate	Bank of America Merrill Lynch	97.03
	Healthcare	Bank of America Merrill Lynch	83.02
	Media and Entertainment	Bank of America Merrill Lynch	81.40
	Consumer Products	Bank of America Merrill Lynch	76.52
	Retail	JP Morgan	52.63
	Governments & Agencies	HSBC Holdings	50.90
	Telecommunications	Lazard	46.61
	Consumer Staples	JP Morgan	40.02

Data from Jan 1 2012 - Mar 28 2012 and Jan 1 2011 - Mar 28 2011   Data as of Mar 28 2012
Regions and Industries table includes fees generated on transactions
excluded from Thomson Reuters' standard league tables.

Banks take these rankings extremely seriously and are very competitive about making it to the Top 3 on every list. Recruiters will expect you to be familiar with these rankings during interviews. If you're determined to work on a certain product or in a particular industry, it helps to check that bank's position within those groups. Since banking is a reputation-based business, clients also pay close attention to who their competitors are hiring to get their deals done. It's a bit of a catch-22; banks that make it to the top book more deals and banks who book more deals make it to the top.

When I was considering which bank to join, J.P. Morgan was #1 in M&A by number of deals generated. As an incoming analyst, I wanted the opportunity to work in a group with high deal flow. I didn't care as much about the size of those deals, so it mattered less to me which bank was ranked highest in total deal value. You will learn just as much from a small multi-million dollar deal than from a large multi-billion dollar deal known in the industry as "elephant" deals.

IV.

Choosing the Best Product and Industry Group For You

"[Industry bankers] build solid, lifelong relations with clients, aiming to service all their banking needs, and tend to cover these clients for life."

Understanding Product Groups

Investment banking is divided into product groups, industry groups, and geographic groups. The three sides work together to meet a client's needs. This is especially common in large, bulge bracket banks.

No matter what your specific interest, once you've been offered a position, you will go through a group selection process where you will rank your group choices from 1 to 10—and the groups will in turn rank you. You will be matched based on your interest level, feedback from your interviews, and your cultural fit. Some banks will give you an offer to directly join a certain group, so it will be even more important that you know exactly which group interests you during the recruiting process. But this is not always the case, so if you have your heart set on joining a particular group, you must network with members of that group and get them to start seeing you as a potential teammate.

The three main product groups are:

1. **Mergers and Acquisitions Advisory (M&A)**

2. **Debt Capital Markets**

3. **Equity Capital Markets**

The product groups work in partnership with industry groups to help execute their deals. For some banks, like Goldman Sachs for example, there is no separate M&A Group—the M&A activities are simply covered by the industry groups. Some banks may have other autonomous groups, such as Risk Management or Syndicated Leverage Finance, but most are organized in these three broad categories. Additionally, within each group, there may be another level of division by types of debt or equity products.

There are many different strategies behind companies' business maneuvers and competitive shifts. If you have ever wondered why a beverage company like PepsiCo. would acquire a chip company like Frito-Lay, or how much it would pay for this acquisition, then a product-focused group like M&A might be the right group for you. If you've always been fascinated by how banks help companies access money through the debt markets, then the Debt Capital Markets team might be a better fit. You'll get to learn about structuring a debt deal, figuring out what interest rate lenders expect for the risk they're taking, how much debt a company can handle, and so on.

The product bankers are considered to be experts at executing. They are familiar with the market dynamics of the product they specialize in and are better positioned to advise a client on things like how much to pay for a target, the right time to issue a bond, how to negotiate the best price on a sale, how to compete against the other potential buyers, how the market will react when you issue the convertible note, etc.

Understanding Industry Groups

Some banks don't cover all industries. If you're interested in working in a specific industry, like the oil and gas industry, it's important to confirm that the banks you are applying to service clients in oil and gas, and excel in that industry group. Size is another factor to take into account: for a major Wall Street firm, groups can be as large as 40 to 100 people per group, depending on the expertise of the bank in that industry.

There are industry groups, also known as "coverage" groups, that cover a list of clients. Some industry groups include:

- **Health Care**

- **Media**

- **Oil and Gas**

- **Real Estate**

- **Financial Sponsors (Private Equity firms or Hedge Funds)**

- **Power and Energy**

- **Consumer Goods**

- **Retail**

- **Financial Institutions**

"Coverage bankers" become experts in the industries they cover, learning the competitive dynamics between different players and when it's a good time to acquire, merge, or sell a division. They also suggest other companies who might be interested in being a potential buyer or partner. Industry group positions are an excellent option for those who are social and sales-oriented. Bankers in these groups become well aware of what's going on in their arena and will have to pitch various ideas to different clients. They build solid, lifelong relations with clients, aiming to service all their banking needs, and tend to cover these clients for life. In turn, clients learn to trust their advice and listen carefully when, for instance, they recommend a good time to issue a bond or bid on a potential acquisition target.

If a client likes the coverage banker's idea, often conveyed through a "pitch," and decides to move forward with the deal, the product team will then tag on to execute the transaction. The deal goes from being a pitch to a "live" transaction.

Having faceted knowledge in one arena can help you when you're trying to determine what industry group you should join. For example, if your parents were doctors, you grew up listening to medical jargon, and you practically had your medical degree out of elementary school, you may know everything there is to know about health care. Knowing the industry well can benefit your career in banking. By joining the health care group, you can combine your strengths into one strong career option.

After you have taken into consideration your passions, knowledge and interests in finance and investment banking, knowing what you're good at can take you far in choosing a product or industry group. And don't forget the leading questions: Are you more social and sales-oriented? Does keeping your finger on the pulse of the market excite you? Are you better at managing longer term projects or shorter ones? There are many similarities between product and industry groups in investment banking, and many times, they work together to execute deals. But there are also differences in the type of deals you'll work on and in the culture of each group. It's up to you to determine which is the best fit for your short-term and long-term career goals.

Selecting the Best Group

To select the right group, I waited until I had accepted my full-time offer and contacted fellow alumni at the bank for help. They then scheduled meetings for me with the various groups that I found most interesting. I remember walking out of the building into the busy streets of Manhattan, exhausted from the long day of meetings, overwhelmed and confused because, in the end, I had liked all of the groups I met with! This was the first sign that I had chosen the right bank. Every group was fascinating in its own way and all of them had a great culture.

Ultimately, I chose the M&A group for four main reasons:

1. It was one of the **more technical groups** at the bank, and I wanted to satisfy my passion for numbers and quantitative analyses.

2. Although I found certain aspects of debt and equity interesting, it was always the **M&A deals that I found most intriguing** when I read business news. I was okay knowing that I would not learn much about pricing a bond or taking a company public during my investment banking career, but that I would learn to master the M&A deal.

3. I was not passionate about a particular industry and was excited by the possibility of becoming what is referred to as a "generalist" at this stage in my career, i.e. someone who gets **exposure to many different industries** rather than focusing on one.

4. I liked the **fun intensity of the group** and felt that my personality connected most with the members of that group, including the Group Head.

V.

The Investment Banking Career Prep Roadmap

"You want to get your feet wet and find out what it is about the various banking positions that excite you, interest you the most, or even what you would be bored to death doing."

Step One: The Internship

The golden ticket to your future career as an investment banker starts with an internship. Trial and error is the best way to find the right career, and interning is the key to unlocking your passions. Since recruiting for internships begins in the fall of your junior year of college (typically starting in November and ending in February) it is wise to begin working on your checklist of requirements early.

The process for applying to be a summer analyst (i.e. intern) or a full-time analyst is largely the same, the differences being that recruiting for full-time positions typically takes place from September to November of your senior year and students are expected to be more knowledgeable. The internship recruiting process is your time to shine: showcase your experience and knowledge and show them that you're light-years ahead of your peers. You definitely want to wow the bankers while being genuine, sincere and honest.

Basic requirements include:

- A **high GPA**,

- Noteworthy **extracurricular activities**, like school clubs and sports, and

- **Networking experience** with alumni and bankers at the banks you are interested in working for.

When it comes to the interview, you can expect at least two rounds. First, there is a **campus interview**, for 12 to 25 students over a day or two. They are usually conducted by alumni on campus, and you may likely be interviewed by two recruiters at the same time for this first round. Come to an interview prepared for the questions you know they will ask, and be sure to include personal information you would like to impart to them. Act the part, both in attire and mannerisms. Most of all, take control of the interview, and show them that you are a perfect fit for the job.

From the initial pool, the recruiters will then select as little as one candidate or as many as five—depending on their need and the quality of the candidates. When I recruited for analyst positions, I once had to make 16 rejection calls and only one invitation for a second round. (The Vice President got to make the invitation and I was stuck with all the rejections!) It was an unpleasant task, but I learned that a bank will never extend second round invitations to students who do not meet the necessary quality standards. **A bank can always find qualified candidates elsewhere.** Don't simply compare yourself to your peers; compare yourself to the entire pool of applicants.

Students who are invited to a second round will typically attend a **"Superday"** at the company's headquarters. The superday interview determines whether you can get the work done and how you stack up against candidates from other schools. The day consists of a morning or afternoon where you will meet one-on-one with four interviewers and enjoy a breakfast or lunch with the other candidates and some bankers. During the downtime before your interview, you will have the opportunity to talk with other candidates and young alumni. This is your last chance to ask any pressing questions you may have before you show off your expertise in finance, banking, and management.

Your interview questions will be tough—the recruiters can smell fear—and you'll begin to wonder if all your hard work was worth it. But when your brow is finally dry after the interview and you land an internship, you're a hop, skip, and a job away from achieving your new career dream. If you got to interview for one of the few full-time openings and landed the position, even better!

Question:

You mentioned that awards, scholarships, and extracurricular activities could help us stand out; what are some specific things that I could put on a resume that would generally catch the eye of a recruiter?

Answer:

As I've stressed before, one of the most attractive things can be showing that you are a top-performing student with strong academics and a high GPA. Specifically, students who serve as Teaching/Research Assistants or who tutor other students at the university would display leadership in academics. Both of these activities mean that a professor or the school administration think you are mature and gifted academically. Membership in honor societies can also help demonstrate this ability.

For extracurricular activities, leadership positions in any activity will make you stand out, whether it is sports, a community service organization, or an industry- focused group. Leadership in a business or finance club can look especially attractive, but you can choose any activity that you are passionate about and it will look equally impressive. If your school doesn't have a finance club or some other club that you would have liked to join, then consider starting it. Being the founder of a school organization shows exceptional leadership, especially if you can share successes from that experience.

Four Tips To Getting Started Early

As a college undergraduate, investment banking recruiters look for a few things when they are considering you for an internship or a job. Before you enter the recruiting process, bulk up on your knowledge of the field and what they will expect you to know. This will help you tremendously in the long run, as will these four tips:

1. Raise Your Hand

Attend every info session held by banking alumni, and come to them with prepared questions or concerns. These alumni are likely also the recruiters for your school, so make sure to listen attentively to their advice and follow it. Try making a good impression by asking a well-prepared question. As always, follow up with a unique and memorable thank you email immediately after the session.

Everyone always recommends that you write handwritten thank you notes. I personally never saw the value in receiving those. They are a nice gesture, but I was always most impressed by students who sent me a well-constructed and typo-free email a few hours after a session ended, rather than ones who sent me a handwritten note days later. By then, I would have already began to make a list of top candidates coming out of the session and the thank-you note arrives too late to make a significant difference.

2. Bon Voyage!

One thing that helped me a lot was my internship at Citigroup during the Boston University London Internship Program in the spring of my junior year; it was an excellent program because it exposed me to different parts of the bank. Take advantage of a study abroad experience that includes an internship and shadow various divisions of banks while you're overseas. The operations of a bank abroad are typically similar enough to the location in the U.S. to make a good assessment.

Even if you're working in another division, you may be able to schedule lunches with investment bankers and learn what they do; shadow portfolio managers to learn more about that side of the business; or you can simply talk shop with commercial bankers and see if their job sparks your interest. You want to get your feet wet and find out what it is about the various positions in a bank that excite you, interest you the most, or even what you would be bored to death doing. All of this can help you prepare stronger responses to why you want to work in investment banking.

3. Bounce Your Ideas Off a Credible Source

Speak to your career counselor. Every school has a career center and they are your best resource, especially since they have known you since your freshman year. They have seen you evolve and know your personality. They're very in tune with recruiters and thus can either gently guide your or tell you flat out, "I don't think this job is a good fit for you or your personality." They can offer you a larger perspective on things you may not have considered or they can affirm your choices and help you make a game plan for recruiting day.

My career counselor Karen played a pivotal role in helping me shape my career vision as an undergraduate. I made it a point to begin fostering this relationship during my first year, so that she saw me through the entire self-discovery process from not being sure what major to choose, to landing my first internship, selecting the right courses for my career goals, and being well-informed about the various career paths available.

She was the one who recommended I attend an info session about investment banking during my second year, one that most students in my year hadn't even heard of! We discussed every trade-off about the job and made sure that it would be a good fit with my personality, my values, and my long-term personal goals. When it was time to interview, she encouraged me to come in and do a mock interview with her. She gave me candid feedback that no one else would have shared, like "**sit closer to the edge of your seat** or you will look un-enthusiastic, even though I know how badly you want this job," and "**don't wear a brown suit**; it's more appropriate to wear a navy or black one for finance jobs."

Career counselors also often develop strong relationships with the recruiters who come to visit the school year after year. If the counselors know you well, they will be your best proponent behind-the-scenes when recruiters discuss potential candidates. They are plugged into what recruiters are looking for, and they are your most accessible resource. They can also become a lifelong mentor, like Karen has been to me, so it's never too late or too early to start building the relationship!

4. Get Personal

It's a good idea to reach out to areas of the bank you are interested in, speak to their personnel and find out about the culture, workload, and specifics of those divisions.

Brainstorm as many avenues as possible so that you have a true sense and understanding of the field and career you're interested in, and see if it feels right. If it doesn't, it probably isn't a good option for you.

When I was at Citigroup, I went to lunch with investment bankers and learned more about what they did—even though my internship was in Asset Management. I was able to compare what excited me between the two functions: asset management, while very interesting, didn't have the fast pace that I loved. Internships that are in closely related fields, or finance in general, will help you understand what motivates you and how you'd like to spend your working days.

Question:

Is it better to reach out to a banker over email or by phone when networking?

Answer:

Generally, emails are a much more appropriate way to reach out to any working professional these days. Calls are usually scheduled in advance or reserved for clients and team members.

I've never received a cold call from an interested student, and I don't believe there are many students who have the confidence to make such a call and the maturity to impress me during that call. If you believe you have both, then making a cold call could make you stand out from the pact. Since you will be interrupting someone's workday, realize that the bar to make a good impression will be set much higher and your plan could backfire if you can't hold your own during the conversation. If you opt for a call over an email, be prepared to swim at your own risk, but potentially catch a big shark!

As a general rule in life, always follow up any voicemails with an email that repeats your message in writing (e.g. "Following up on my voicemail, I can be reached at…"). When I would spend my day in meetings or on calls, I used to check my emails more frequently than my voicemails. It is becoming increasingly faster in the business world to receive a response through email rather than by phone.

What Recruiters Look For

Recruiters look for specific talents and strengths in their recommended interns and job candidates. Banks are traditional and conservative organizations that aren't going to veer from their proven formula of recruiting. They are looking for the best of the best in the world, and they tend to bring in candidates using the same channels each year. If you don't happen to be in one of these channels, you can still get in—but it's a lot harder, and you will need to network, network, network!

Ivy League Plus

Recruiters mainly pull from the top schools: think Harvard, Stanford, and MIT. Each bank has a list of core schools where they actively recruit, coordinated through dedicated Human Resources teams at the bank. There are also acceptable non-core schools that students can be hired from, coordinated by alumni bankers. Together, these two groups of schools make up the list of institutions that bankers are allowed to hire from.

If you're not at one of the schools on the list, don't worry, you can still get into banking. It just means that you will have to work harder and that the odds might be lower. You can try networking, but sometimes even if you get your resume into the hands of a seasoned banker, they might not be able to get it past H.R. The best course of action at that point is to start at a boutique firm and try to transition from there, or get into a top business school and apply with an MBA.

From year to year, the list of recruited schools may also change. For instance, during boom years, more schools get dedicated recruiting teams and a budget. In recessionary years, a lot of schools will get cut, but alumni bankers are still encouraged to recruit at those schools; they just have to do it on their own dime and are expected to only take up a superday interview spot if the candidate is exceptional. When I was at BU, I went through a formal recruiting process on campus. But not all the top banks recruited actively there (i.e. the school wasn't on every bank's core list), so I had to be proactive and reach out to a few others on my own through networking and speaking to alumni working at those firms.

Another option is to crash banking events held at other schools. Although some schools may not appreciate this, I've had success stories with candidates who were so passionate about banking that they would attend recruiting events at other universities and network with recruiters that way. I've had a number of candidates approach me from neighboring schools when I recruited at Harvard. It showed how committed they were to pursuing investment banking, which is top of mind for every recruiter. If you are a strong candidate, which means you know the ins and outs of banking, you can certainly impress a recruiter at one of these events and catch their attention for further discussions.

If you're going to crash an event, it's important that you present yourself at the same caliber as the other students there—otherwise, you will make yourself look bad in front of the recruiter, and they won't take you seriously. The best way to do this is to partner with friends studying at another university. Check your resume with them in advance, and simply tag along to their event! Banks like to see friends working together through the recruiting process; it shows teamwork and a collaborative spirit.

Stellar Grades

The higher, the better when it comes to your GPA. For undergraduates, most banks will list a formal cutoff of 3.2 in their application requirements, but a 3.5 is the informal norm. In some circumstances, you can get an internship with a 3.2 or above, but it is typically because you've networked and shown that you can nail every single banking question, or because you stood out on your resume through relevant work experience.

Some other extras that can help you bulk up your academic portfolio and set you apart are:

- Honors

- Scholarships

- Awards

- A strong foundation in finance or accounting

Ambitious and Proven

Any previous related finance, accounting, or economics experience is helpful. It helps if you held a past internship with a recognized brand name company, because it shows that you were a strong enough candidate to get through that difficult selection process. It's just another filter that proves you've already made the cut.

If you can't find an internship in finance or accounting, look for a business development *finance, if there are no bankers).*

- *This will involve a cold call or email. Ask the alumnus for a short informational phone call, or meeting if you live nearby. Referring to the session as "informational" rather than an interview is important as it implies you don't expect to get a job out of this relationship.*

- *Make sure to keep your initial email or call short. Introduce yourself, let them know about your interest in their field, and ask for the informational chat. If you've heard or read anything about the alumnus, you can also mention it briefly. Any correspondence more than a few sentences may cause a delay in response time or no response at all, so aim for brevity.*

- *Be prepared to sound intelligent if you are reaching out to a senior alumni, but also don't be afraid! They are the decision-makers so getting in with the senior team members can pay off hugely.*

3) Ask Finance/Business professors for any advice and contacts.

- *Even if they're not your professors, ask to meet with them and use the meeting to show that you are capable and professional. Some of them may have even worked in the field before teaching and still have connections with recruiters. Others may have authored relevant case studies or consulted companies that are of interest to you.*

- *Regardless of whether they can share contacts, professors are aware of the latest trends in the field and can help prepare you for your informational and recruiting interviews. I solicited the help of my Finance professor when preparing for my interviews; the advice he gave me on what topics to mention in my answers had a direct result on me getting the job.*

4) Ask your peers if they have any family friends in the field or if they know anyone who recently graduated and is now working in Banking or Finance. Recent graduates will be your BEST resource and connection. Professors and career coaches may know about these recent graduates too, so also ask them for names.

5) Join your school's Finance Club to build relationships with guest speakers and club sponsors. If your school doesn't have a finance club, consider starting one. It's a great way to reach out to alumni and industry professionals under the premise of "I'm President/Founder of the Finance Club". You can invite alumni to come speak about their company or their careers, solicit the advice of a banker on a company valuation that the club is working on, or ask if you can visit their company in an organized trip to Wall Street. Note that bulge bracket firms have strict guidelines about organized trips and may refer you to their H.R. department, so try to think creatively about making a request that can be fulfilled depending on whom you're reaching out to. Either way, use your leadership in the Finance Club as an opening to connect with a banker and build a relationship.

VI.

Advice For Career Switchers

"If the light bulb has gone off and you're planning the departure from your current career field, you're not dreaming an impossible dream."

When You're Not Already On the Banking Track

The investment banking bug has bitten you, eh? If the light bulb has gone off and you're planning the departure from your current career field, you're not dreaming an impossible dream. It will, however, take some serious networking and cultivating of relationships within the industry, as well as a great deal of hard work and research to be done *before* you begin school. It's best if you start cultivating the relationships a full six months prior to the start of the school year.

The economic downturn has affected the hiring process; in some years banks will recruit for full-time positions as well as internships, and in other years they may only hire from their pools of interns. Keep in mind: they may drop recruiting for full-time associates, but they will never drop recruiting for summer associates. Therefore, it's imperative that you work on your internship prospects as early in your MBA or JD career as possible to ensure that you land an internship the summer between your first and second year of school. Getting an internship is sometimes your only chance to get into banking out of graduate school, as many of the top firms don't return in the fall for full-time recruiting.

For banks that do both internship and full-time recruiting, the process is virtually the same. Besides timing, the only other difference is that recruiters will ask a lot more questions about your summer internship if you're applying to a full-time position in your second year. They will want to understand why you weren't able to get an internship in banking if that's what you wanted, why you're changing your mind now, what you learned during your summer that is transferable, etc.

Once you are ready to apply for an associate position, it isn't as easy as going online and filling out an application to the bank of your choice. In fact, the online application is not worth a lot and is relevant only in your Human Resources file. Your resume, and possibly your cover letter, are the meat and potatoes of your experience; you should put a lot of thought, emphasis, and shining moments into these items.

I've had many students come up to me during recruiting season feeling overwhelmed. Yes, it's true that most of the banks will be on campus recruiting at business schools around the same time. The good news it that you can typically replicate your applications from one bank to another, so you can easily apply to many. What you can't replicate is networking, one of the most essential elements of your application. And keeping track of all the people you're meeting will be difficult! It helps to commit names to memory or write them down somewhere, so that you can reference the right individuals when you're trying to mention meeting them in another conversation or in an interview.

But while recruiters expect you to be applying to multiple firms, it's important to be extra-organized throughout the process. At recruiting dinners, I've had students walk out halfway through the meal to attend another bank's dinner. Avoid being so obvious: **Each bank wants to feel that they are your top choice**, so you have to manage your commitments (interviews, dinners, etc.) delicately.

Typically, about 20 to 30 students will be selected for an interview on campus. These will take place over the course of one or two days, sometimes at a nearby hotel. The recruiting team will then invite a subset of those students for second-round interviews, which typically consist of two more interviews, also on campus or sometimes at company headquarters. The second-round interviews will get more technical and may include a case study or modeling exercise.

Question:

I am finishing my PhD in a language program, but have decided that I'd like to go into Investment Banking; do you have any advice on how I can do this?

Answer:

If you are interested in moving into investment banking with your background, I think you will need to consider non-traditional paths to break into the industry. As mentioned in the book, the "typical" paths for getting into Wall Street usually involve following a very rigid undergraduate or graduate degree in business or a related field and attending recruiting events at top universities. In your case, given that you are in a PhD program, those opportunities will unfortunately not be available to you. However, I think you could start by targeting smaller boutique firms that are more open to candidates from non-traditional backgrounds. You can search the web for a listing of firms in your area. The key to your landing a business/finance job will be networking, so try to reach out to professors at your university, fellow alumni, or friends/family for introductions.

The other option for you is to think about how you can leverage your existing skill sets and apply them to a position in business/finance. In your case, it may make sense to seek out firms that need a bilingual team member. These firms may be either based in the

U.S. with a group that focuses on a market abroad (almost every major bank has such a group) or in country abroad doing business with the U.S. If you prove to them that you understand some finance (from taking a course or doing your own research) and that you are a quick learner, they might be willing to teach you the rest in order to leverage your language skills.

If you are 100% set on switching to business/finance, then one of the most certain options would be to go back to school and get an MBA. I know that given your strong educational background, this may seem like a lengthy and costly option, but there were students in my MBA program who had PhD's, so I mention this for your consideration. It would be the most structured way to make a transition.

Tips for MBA & JD Applicants

1. **Your best resources are your peers who previously worked in the field.**

As a graduate student, you have the benefit of having former bankers living and breathing right next to you—so take advantage of this special access! Many of them are likely still in regular contact with their former employers, and may even play a role in the selection of candidates.

I spent a lot of time during the first few months at Harvard Business School meeting with students who were thinking of applying to banking. They would reach out to me and schedule short coffee breaks or lunches. I also held an event to prep students who were applying. Look out for these types of events and socialize with the other students who are planning to apply.

When at J.P. Morgan, many business school students would travel to our offices together and schedule meetings on the same day. It showed their enthusiasm and ability to collaborate with each other. Partnering with a friend to tackle the application process can help significantly and ensure that you don't miss anything important.

2. **Get to recruiting events extra early to gain a networking advantage.**

One of the best and easiest ways to network at recruiting events, and to show your strong interest, is to get there early! Not just a few minutes early—I'm talking 15-30 minutes early. In the worst case scenario, you'll have to wait for the event to begin.

When recruiting at Harvard, I used to fly in from New York with fellow recruiters and often arrive at least an hour before start time to set up and get organized. The students who stuck out the most were the ones who would eagerly show up extremely early before I got swarmed by the sea of other candidates. There will probably be on average one recruiter for every 5-10 students, so getting your individual voice heard will be difficult. Showing up early can change that ratio to one-to-one!

3. **The culture of a bank can either make or break your experience.**

It is very important that you look at all aspects of a potential bank job, including cultural fit. If you're highly competitive and you are considering a bank that discourages competition among peers, you're probably not going to fit in too well at a bank that evaluates you based on collaboration. Some banks might also promote cultures that are more aggressive than others. I chose J.P. Morgan because I felt that it valued integrity and inclusiveness above making profit, two qualities that I value deeply in my personal life. Pay attention to the cultural vibes and make sure they match your own.

Question:

I attend a school where it is incredibly difficult to find students who share the same aspirations/ambitions as me in pursuing Investment Banking; do you know how I can find like-minded peers?

Answer:

There are three things you can do to find a peer group:

1) If your school doesn't already have a finance club, consider starting one. This is by far the best way to rally students with a similar interest. Look at the websites of finance clubs at other schools to learn of the types of activities you can organize (speaker events, conferences, panels, career workshops, valuation exercises, Excel tutorials, company visits, trip to Wall Street, etc.).

2) Check out Wall Street Oasis. It has an active discussion board where you can post a new question/topic and solicit feedback from the community. Also, http://www.mergersandinquisitions.com is a good blog with many resources for getting into banking. You can read through the "Recruiting" tab, but if any of the advice you find there conflicts with mine, then you already know what my recommendation would be!

3) You can crash events at other schools to begin making friends. Sometimes, you'll find finance conferences that are open to a number of schools. This is particularly true for minorities or women. For instance, I was invited to speak at an "85 Broads" Conference in Boston that was open to students from 35 chapters worldwide. You can look up these annual events and use them as an opportunity to network with peers and bankers alike. You can also reach out to friends at other universities (e.g. old friends from high school) and see if you can join any school-specific events as an observer or join their working group.

What Recruiters Look For: MBA & JD Applicants

At the Associate level, **relevant work experience, strong personality,** and **commitment to banking** matter most.

If you are at a strong graduate school, there will be almost no focus on your academics. Instead, for an associate applicant coming from a top business or law school, the first thing that recruiters will look at is your prior work experience. You will get a gold star in your interviews for previous finance, accounting, and consulting experience. These fields are closely related to the job and will act as a strong platform for your launch into investment banking. If your experience is in an unrelated field, that can still be attractive —especially fields that are analytical or quantitative like engineering. Recruiters will want to know whether you worked for a strong company, performed exceptionally well, and tackled high levels of responsibility. All these qualities would imply that you are of associate caliber.

If your experience got a check on the list of requirements, the next thing you will have to convey is your complete and utter focus on pursuing a career in banking. You will have to convince recruiters that you've had a serious change of heart and are ready to make the switch if your previous career is unrelated. To do this, you'll need to sound like all of the other candidates who actually did work in a related field. Your main objective will be to showcase your deep understanding of banking and finance. The best way to do this is to take as many finance courses possible, read business publications regularly, and network with bankers.

If you're still raring to go on this new venture, and you've stopped reading this only to sign up for a Top 10 business school, you will need to work on your internship checklist as soon as you get admitted. During periods of economic slow-down, banks may not be back on campus in your second year to recruit for full-time positions, so put your energy into getting that internship! You need to be ready to jump in the summer between your first and second year of school. If you work hard, you'll come back to your second year with a full-time offer in hand a nice sign-on bonus.

Getting into investment banking may feel daunting if you've held a career outside of finance, but chances are your previous experiences have prepared you for an associate level investment banking job. The combination of your previous career experience, graduate degree from a top institution, and a nice web of contacts in the industry will help you reset your career and get you on the right foot to becoming a banker. If you feel confident that you can enter the industry jogging, not walking, then it's time to lace up your running shoes and get going on building up your contacts and knowledge.

Expectations of an Associate Over an Analyst

You've started networking with various banks and your job applications have been submitted. Now what? If you're ready to start preparing for job interviews, there are a few areas you should concentrate on for an associate level investment banking job that differ from those of the undergraduate applicants. These may be tougher qualities to find in a young undergrad and are more easily excused, but they are non-negotiables for anyone applying to an Associate position.

Maturity

Recruiters seek a different level of maturity in associates than they do in analysts. Recruiters will ask themselves questions like: "Can I put this person in front of a Fortune 500 company CEO and know for certain that they can run the meeting?" or "Can this person manage a delicate analyst issue with discretion and grace?" Associates are older, and are expected to actually act older. You will be expected to be vocal, when appropriate. An analyst rarely speaks at an important client meeting and most just observe, but associates often have speaking roles. Recruiters will test you to make sure that you can come to meetings prepared to talk and defend your work.

The behavioral questions of the interview will also be more managerial in nature. Associates are counted on to give feedback to analysts and serve as the eyes and ears of the Managing Director. If there is an issue on the deal team or with the client, the associate is expected to escalate it appropriately and maturely.

You will also be assessed on how you handle yourself in tricky or unethical situations. For instance, you may get a question like, "what would you do if you found out the numbers are incorrect minutes before a client meeting?" There is not one right answer, but there is definitely a wrong one, and the process will be designed to weed out individuals who would act naively.

Long-Term Commitment

During your interviews, there will be significant focus on your life story: "Why exactly did that light bulb go on in your head, convincing you there was no other job in the world for you but investment banking?" You should definitely be prepared to answer the hard questions about choices you've made thus far (with little fluff) and provide honest and sincere explanations. The recruiters—and ultimately, the bank—are looking for candidates who want to make a lifelong career out of banking.

I've seen students apply and then share stories of their passion for start ups during the interview—that's not an appropriate interest if you're applying to be an associate. No one wants to hear that you're using this job as a stepping stone to make big bonuses, save money, and then start your own business someday (although it definitely happens!). They are looking for applicants that have career goals past the associate level and are eager to climb the ladder to upper levels of management, like a vice president or managing director. At this higher level, recruiters want to know that you want to make a career out of investment banking.

It is understood that analysts will most likely stay for only two years and then move on to join a private equity firm, a hedge fund, the corporate development group of a client, or apply to business school. On the other hand, associates are expected to stay on permanently, or at least be open to the idea of rising through the ranks and running the group someday. So whether you're single or married with kids, you have to show your eagerness to do the hard work and hold on during the tough times. I had a married candidate once mention that his wife was fully supportive of his interest in banking and was aware that his schedule will be unpredictable. It helped reinforce that he had the right expectations about banking and the support of his family to launch this long-term career path on the right foot.

Project Management

As a banking analyst, you can come in, work hard, learn and progress into an associate position after two to three years. If you're an MBA hoping to come in at the associate level, you need to be prepared to take the job by the horns. You must not only demonstrate to upper-management that you can be the glue that holds the team together, but you have to be mentally, physically, and emotionally prepared to do that despite the long hours.

When I recruited potential associates from Harvard, one of the most important qualities we looked for in a strong MBA candidate was the ability to manage the entire deal team with minimal supervision. We looked for candidates who could meet the demands of senior team members, supervise junior team members, and manage client expectations on multiple deals at a time, typically 3 to 5 deal teams at any given point. The ability to manage work flow with precision and delegate effortlessly are highly desired assets.

Stronger Technical Knowledge

From a technical perspective, you will be expected to know more than an analyst. There will be room for job training on Wall Street, but you need to prove that you can learn quickly and that you're proactive. You have to show you've studied finance in greater detail and can explain the rationale underlying financial or accounting concepts.

You need to show them that though it's been two years since your middle-management gig, you did your homework about banking and have a strong grasp of the current financial construct, as well as the various analyses you'll do on the job. After all, you may need to teach these concepts to an analyst on one of your future teams. If you can't verbalize it succinctly in an interview, chances are you won't be able to explain it to an analyst either. You will also be asked to build a simple model or analyze a case study.

VII.

Resources For Applicants

"If you find yourself bored when reading about deals, then banking may not be for you."

Online Bookmarks For Application Reading

You've done the research, spoken to bankers, and decided to pursue a job in investment banking. You now need to get smart on the industry to make sure you can impress your prospective employers and nail those tough interview questions. You're going to need to do a little research to get fully prepared.

There are vast resources online, where you can read more about investment banking jobs, requirements, and current news on the industry. They help to get you in the right mindset for the recruiting process. They're also helpful to read when you're prepping for interviews to make sure that you're thinking along the right lines. I have also found that daily deal sites (such as the Daily Deal and The New York Times Deal Book) are thorough sites for industry news and commentary. Browsing through these sites regularly will help to ensure that you are kept abreast of the latest industry trends. If you find yourself bored when reading about deals, then banking may not be for you. You may get asked during interviews to share details about deals that you find interesting. For my interviews, I found it much easier to respond to such questions since I had been regularly browsing these two sources and was in the loop on the status of deals being announced on the street.

Sites like The New York Times Deal Book help you to see the impact of macro events on the banking world. Associates, more than analysts, will be expected to understand the implications of current events on the banking industry since they are pursuing this as a life-long career. Analysts may also be asked about trends in banking and what this means for future deal flow. While *The Wall Street Journal* is always a good resource for such knowledge, the Deal Book helps to tie the latest news directly to the banking sector.

A more academic resource on corporate finance and valuation, NYU Professor Aswath Damodaran' teaches a module in the training programs of many of the top Wall Street banks. I found him to be extremely engaging and helpful when he taught my training class. One of the most unique pieces of advice he shared with us at the end of the week was "to always remember that we have the 'option to abandon.'"

This is an oft-forgotten concept used in finance when discussing "real options." It represents the value of being able to exit an unsuccessful project rather than keep losing money on it. I think he was trying to tell us that we can always pursue another job if we are unhappy for any reason in banking. Sometimes, it's easy to lose sight of that and feel trapped in whatever job you choose. It was an empowering lesson, and a good one to keep in mind as you explore all your career options!

Below, you'll find a complete aggregation of my collected online resources for investment banking applicants:

- Vault **(http://www.vault.com/)**

  The Vault offers "career intelligence" for seekers. It's a comprehensive site filled with industry information, rankings, banking information, and cover letter and resume tips. They have helpful guides on investment banking jobs and finance interviews.

- Wet Feet **(http://www.wetfeet.com/)**

  Wet Feet is a rich site filled with hundreds of advice articles, insider information on employers, and tips for networking. The quick links to job interviews, resume tips, and job search information is especially helpful as an investment banking resource.

- Jargon Buster **(http://careers.jpmorgan.com/)**

  Every bank shares resources for interested candidates on its website as well as a calendar of upcoming recruiting events. The J.P. Morgan advice center includes a "Jargon Buster" section, a list of commonly used banking terms and their definitions. Reading through this will help in your interview preparation.

- The Daily Deal **(http://www.thedeal.com)**

  The Daily Deal offers insider information on M&A, private equity, hedge funds, and more. This site includes daily news and current affairs, as well industry opinions, job listings, and career advice. It's an outstanding resource for all industry related topics.

- NYT Deal Book **(http://dealbook.nytimes.com)**

  This New York Times site is a strong resource on banking, M&A, IPO's, and private equity. The site offers sections on various banking sectors and a live wire ticker of industry news and advice.

- Investment Valuation by Aswath Damodaran **(http://www.damodaran.com)**

If you don't want to purchase textbooks by Professor Aswath Damodaran, or want to get a taste for his teaching style first, he has created an excellent and free website of his materials and corporate finance lessons. He also has a great blog.

Recommended Investment Banking Reading List

Even in the rapidly advancing technological age, newspapers and industry publications are popular among industry bankers and business leaders. When it comes to a career in banking, your investment banking reading list is a necessary means to staying plugged in with changing news and shifting landscapes. Keeping up on industry changes, history, news, and even humor, is one way you can continuously improve your game and career as an investment banker.

In addition to reading *The Wall Street Journal* and other newspapers, you should take the time to read full-length books which offer an in-depth look at the banking industry. These specific titles referenced below are from my personal reading list, that I recommend you read to fill any weak spots in your preparation

The Day the Economy Slumped

Market reads are ripe with bad reputation stories centering on the economic crash and the subprime mortgage crisis. After the slump in 2008, books on what happened during the crisis, and who is to blame, have hit the shelves in droves.

For newcomers to the industry, reading various viewpoints about the government's interference and the regulation of the banks can be enlightening and useful. After the subprime mortgage crisis, Bear Stearns collapsed, Lehman Brothers filed for bankruptcy, and a few others were acquired by competing banks. If you're interested in investment banking, you need to thoroughly understand the economic collapse.

Suggested Reading: *Fool's Gold* by Gillian Tett

Wait, Banking is Fun?

It's not all about hard news, bad news and breaking financial stories. There are fun reads on the market that you can thoroughly enjoy once you've been in the business for awhile.

Reading books like this will give you an insider's look, with a little added humor, on banking jobs and what is really asked and required of them.

A well-known industry favorite, often recommended to those entering the business or interested in it, is *Monkey Business.* As industry jargon goes, investment bankers are often called monkeys because they are working all the time, following instructions and not doing a lot of thinking on their own.

Suggested Reading:

- *Monkey Business: Swinging through the Wall Street Jungle* by John Rolfe and Peter Troob

- *Barbarians at the Gate: The Fall of RJR Nabisco* by Bryan Burrough and John Helyar

- *Bank* by David Bledin

Finance is Not Rocket Science

Students always ask me what they can do to better prepare for the technical interview questions or for the internship. You do not need to know how to build a model for either, but some understanding of financial concepts will certainly be required. Reading textbooks may be one of the best ways to solidify the financial theories that get applied in the investment banking world. Don't get caught up in the details, but it is important to have a general comprehension of corporate finance.

Suggested Reading:

- *Investment Banking: Valuation, Leveraged Buyouts, and Mergers and Acquisitions* by Josh Rosenbaum, Josh Pearl, Joseph Perella — Describes the practice of valuation in the real world

- *The Practitioner's Guide to Investment Banking, Mergers & Acquisitions, and Corporate Finance* by Jerilyn Castillo and Peter McAniff — More focused on M&A concepts than leveraged buyouts, debt, or equity

- *Investment Valuation* by Aswath Damodaran — Explains the theory behind valuation concepts

Other Titles of Value

- *Vault Career Guide to Investment Banking*

Building your reading list and staying on top of current news and events will make the difference between simply answering interview questions and answering questions well. In short, a strong understanding of current, financial and world news will strengthen your chances of landing an investment banking job.

VIII

Investment Banking Resumes

"A recruiter will spend about one minute going over your resume, so your strongest attributes and experiences need to stand out."

Five Tips To Make Your Resume Stand Out

Creating a compelling and persuasive investment banking resume can lift you above the pack and guarantee an interview. Since investment banking is extremely competitive and the jobs are in high demand, your experience, knowledge and resume need to be ahead of your peers.

A recruiter will spend about one minute going over your resume, so your strongest attributes and experiences need to stand out. As always, **attention to detail is crucial.**

There are a couple of items recruiters will look at first when they receive your resume. For analyst positions, your GPA needs to meet the quota of 3.5. Failure to meet this minimum can automatically put your resume in the "Maybe" pile. For associates, provided you're already coming from a top business school, your MBA academics will matter less. Recruiters will glance at your undergraduate record but pay the most attention to your prior work experience, your previous role, and how these translate to a banking associate position.

At the very least, your resume should be one page, easy to scan quickly, and featuring compelling information that jumps off the page. Your margins should be no less than half an inch; your font should be a standard font (such as Times New Roman or Arial) and a regular size (no less than 10 point). To make your resume rise to the top of the pile, review these five tips:

1. **Pick Two to Three of Your Strongest Experiences.**

Since your resume is looked over quickly, you need to showcase your strongest experiences right away. Pick two or three of your strongest experiences and feature them near the top of your resume. Analysts' resumes need to highlight their academic strengths, honors, awards, and any previous internship experience. If you're applying for your first internship, the recruiters will assess you based on your academic accomplishments and leadership in your extracurriculars. Associate resumes need to highlight work, any internships, and any experience related to finance.

2. **Use the Correct Format.**

Your investment banking resume has a different focus than a resume for a job in another industry. It should highlight analytical and quantitative abilities above any other qualities that you may value in yourself (such as being creative, entrepreneurial, or tech-savvy). Make sure you focus on results, and convey any recognition you received for achieving those results. If you have prior experience in the field, you should list deal experience by deal amount and client name, then follow it with a brief account of your role on the transaction (e.g. what types of analyses did you work on, who were the players that you interacted with, etc.).

To ensure that the basic format is in line with your peers, make sure to check with your career office for the school's acceptable resume format. Every school has its own look; you will seem unprepared if your resume is the only one in the pile that doesn't match the look of the others. It will mean that you haven't consulted a career coach throughout the process, and that you're not taking advantage of your school's resources. Recruiters know and respect the staff at the career offices so it's in your best interest to follow their advice carefully.

3. **Know the Mistakes to Avoid the Mistakes.**

Generic information. Flat descriptions. No results. These are some of the biggest mistakes found in banking resumes. If you give the impression that you didn't fully understand what you did in your previous job, what does this say about your competence and capacity to learn?

For example, after you list an internship, you include that you compiled reports for acquisitions. Okay—what does that really mean? Did you understand what you were doing? What kind of reports? What acquisitions? Be specific. Use bullet points. Highlight the results you achieved and how you got there. Discuss any big projects you were involved in, the length of time they ran, the specific sections you handled, or how you worked on a team and what you contributed to it.

4. **Think Outside the Box But Stay Inside the Lines**.

Take a look at your resume. If it's not focused with detailed, concise bullet points, the bulk of your resume may be irrelevant and is just taking up space. Specificity is worth more than long sentences that don't add much value to your candidacy.

If you're an undergrad, you may not have a lot of experience to highlight. Instead, showcase other activities where you've had to take on responsibility. Are you involved in a club or sport? Have you been volunteering for years outside of school? Are you a Resident Assistant? If you've had any academic achievements, recruiters know those also take time, hard work, and dedication to attain, so make sure to list all of them. List only achievements from high school that were truly extraordinary: a near-perfect score on your SAT's, a high class rank, or a national spelling bee championship. Otherwise, leave high school off the resume and in your memories.

If you're an MBA student, don't worry about listing all your past experiences. Some of the older ones, like internships in college, may no longer fit on the page or are no longer relevant. Focus on fleshing out your more recent and related experience instead.

5. **Typo? No Job.**

There is no room for mistakes in your resume. As will all components of your application, you have to demonstrate a high attention to detail. It needs to be polished, focused and offer a brilliant representation of all that you have achieved or are working on. Check to make sure that the formatting and spacing in your resume is consistent. If you're ending bullets with periods, make sure there's one at the end of every bullet (unless it's a list of short items). You will be amazed how detail-oriented bankers are and how ticked off the slightest mistake can make them. Show them that you, too, care about the little stuff.

Once you've finished writing, editing and proofreading your resume, pass it around to a few friends. Watch how they read it, see where they get caught up, and ask for their honest feedback. Then edit, proofread, read, repeat. You are striving for perfection here, so it could take several rounds of edits.

Resume Sample

Donna Khalife
[Address] [Email Address] [Phone Number]

Education

2009-2011 **HARVARD BUSINESS SCHOOL**

Master in Business Administration. Awarded John H. McArthur Fellowship. Elected Section Officer. Published HBS case on Social Entrepreneurship. Contestant in Business Plan Competition. Attended two-week program in Vietnam on emerging markets. Member of Entrepreneurship, Media, Middle East, and Social Enterprise Clubs.

2001-2005 **BOSTON UNIVERSITY**   **BOSTON, MA**

Bachelor of Science in Business Administration, concentration in Finance, *summa cum laude*. Bachelor of Arts in International Relations, *magna cum laude*. University Scholar. Dean's List. Lead Probability and Statistics teaching assistant. Founder and co-President of the B.U. Lebanese Club. Actor in theatre productions.

spring 2004 **BOSTON UNIVERSITY STUDY ABROAD PROGRAM**   **LONDON, ENGLAND**

Internship at Citigroup Asset Management. Academic focus on International Economics.

Experience

summer 2010 **GRAMEEN AMERICA (U.S. chapter of Grameen Bank in Bangladesh)**   **NEW YORK, NY**
Summer Associate

Start-up microfinance firm founded by Nobel Laureate Dr. Muhammad Yunus to alleviate poverty in the U.S. Launched a new website and implemented a grassroots campaign to increase online traffic and brand awareness.

2005-2009 **J.P. MORGAN SECURITIES**   **NEW YORK, NY**
Mergers and Acquisitions Associate (promoted from Analyst in June 2008)

Analyzed and executed strategic transactions (mergers, acquisitions, divestitures, joint ventures, and minority investments) for clients across multiple industries, including media, healthcare, industrials, retail, and power.

Project Management

- Promoted to senior analyst and to associate; awarded highest performance ranking every year (top 10%)
- Worked extensively with management teams of Fortune 500 companies to evaluate investments, conduct due diligence, create confidential selling materials, and negotiate with counterparties.
- Managed multiple teams of 3-5 people simultaneously and led external teams of lawyers, co-advisors, accountants, and counterparties to execute transactions efficiently and maximize benefit to client.
- Attended several Board and executive meetings and participated in key strategy decision-making.
- Supervised potential buyers on their site visits to over 20 global facilities across a number of industries.

Analytics

- Significant experience in valuing businesses through discounted cash flow, leveraged buyout, sum-of-the-parts, trading comparables, and precedent comparable transactions analyses.
- Performed complex financial analyses to determine the impact of a transaction (merger modeling, synergies analysis, value creation for shareholders, accretion/dilution analysis, and relative contribution analysis).

Selected Transaction Experience

- Multi-billion dollar sale of The Weather Channel and www.weather.com to NBC, Bain, and Blackstone
- R.H.Donnelley's $9.7 billion acquisition of Dex Media
- GM/Chrysler government bailout
- $1.5 billion divestiture of Goodyear's Engineered Products Division to The Carlyle Group

Organizational Leadership

- Selected by Group Head to be a member of the J.P. Morgan *Junior Women in Banking* Operating Committee.
- Big Brothers Big Sisters volunteer (since 2005); created a J.P. Morgan Workplace Mentoring Program to mentor underprivileged girls in New York; helped raise $25,000 for New York City's "Race for the Kids".
- Active in undergraduate and post-MBA recruiting; member of the Harvard and B.U. recruiting teams.
- Trained analysts and associates; designed and led a course on "Attention to Detail".

spring 2004 **CITIGROUP ASSET MANAGEMENT**   **LONDON, ENGLAND**
Analyst Intern

Created reports tracking the performance of Citi mutual funds; reports were distributed to clients worldwide.

Personal   Fluent in French and Arabic (citizenship in U.S., Canada, and Lebanon). Series 7 and 63 licenses. Enjoy traveling (traveled to more than 25 countries), biking, mentoring, online start-ups, and the performing arts.

IX

Investment Banking Cover Letters

". . . cover letters in banking are rarely read. Truthfully, they almost don't matter. Almost. If they're poorly written or have typos, they could cost you the interview."

Does Your Cover Letter Matter?

You've probably heard that cover letters are the strongest representation of yourself when you're applying for a job. In fact, there have been new reports since the downturn of the economy that when you're constructing your cover letter, you have to think that you're going up against hundreds of applicants for one job. It's all about catching the eye of the recruiter with a stellar piece of literature right from the first line. You have to stand out in all the right ways for your shot at an interview.

However, this isn't the case when you're applying for an analyst or associate level position in banking. When it comes down to how you craft your investment banking cover letter, highlighting your experiences and qualifications won't do you much good! In fact, it almost doesn't matter what you say or showcase about yourself, because cover letters in banking are rarely read. Truthfully, they almost don't matter. Almost. If they're poorly written or have typos, they could cost you the interview. So this doesn't mean you don't need to include one with your application, and it certainly doesn't give you a pass to put just anything on it.

When I was applying, I wrote a cover letter and used nine-point font because there were so many things I had done and wanted to say. The truth is, when I was on the inside, we rarely looked at cover letters! However, there will be some recruiters that love them because **they add a human touch** to your resume. Therefore, it's important to create a focused cover letter that sings about specific qualifications, interests, or experiences your resume doesn't include.

1. **K.I.S.S.**

The most effective writing pneumonic out there: Keep It Short and Simple. When you're writing your cover letter, you want to make sure it's short, to the point and concise. Ideally, you want to get across points that your resume doesn't already include, reflecting two to three things that show how committed you are to banking and what makes you the right candidate. Just repeating your resume in full sentences does not equate a cover letter.

2. **Complement Your Resume**.

Your cover letter should aim to add value beyond your resume. Use it to highlight specific strengths your resume doesn't detail or to further expand upon your extracurricular activities. Hopefully, you've written an excellent resume and there isn't much to add—that's great! It gives you room to explain precisely why you want this position or this bank. Be specific; generic cover letters are very easy to spot. If you've met with people at the bank, say so and share what you took from those conversations. Be creative and use the cover letter as a way to introduce yourself without repeating yourself.

3. **Who Are You?**

There are a lot of different angles you could take in constructing your cover letter. For example: maybe you listed internships in your resume, but you didn't get to fully explain what you took away from those internships, or what you really enjoyed that relates to a position in banking. How are your experiences relevant to who you are and what do they mean for your career in investment banking?

4. **Address the Obvious Questions.**

Most times in banking applications, the cover letter is reviewed after the resume. Thus, the cover letter can provide insight on questions the resume raises. For instance, if your resume features amazing work experience in an Investment Bank, but your GPA is low, recruiters will wonder, "What happened here?" Your cover letter should shed some light on why your academics took a hit. However, you should only do so if your GPA is truly low. Reading about why a candidate ended up with a 3.4 instead of a 3.6 is a waste of time and will make you seem immature.

You can also ask yourself, "will something on my resume be misinterpreted?" If so, this is the place to explain anything that needs explaining. Your cover letter could be a great way to expound on the experiences that helped shape who you are. Just remember to **keep it relevant**. You don't want to pour your heart out if it doesn't make sense for the job. But remember: some recruiters won't make it to the cover letter, so ideally you should try to address any open questions directly on your resume.

When I was applying to banking in the beginning of my Senior year, recruiters kept asking me why I hadn't done an internship the summer before. The last internship I had listed on my resume was the one at Citigroup, which was from the second semester of my Junior year. I thought it would have been enough, but the summer gap in my resume made them feel uncomfortable.

I had actually done a lot during that summer but I didn't include it because I thought it didn't fit the mold of the resume. I had accepted a major finance internship that was canceled a week before I was scheduled to start due to budget constraints. The summer had begun and it was too late to get another internship, so I took college courses in finance and other subjects to make use of my time. They liked my response and said it should have been on the resume. Once I added the explanation under my most recent work experience, it never came up again in another interview. You could explain unusual things in your cover letter, but you should always try to find a spot for them somewhere on your resume first.

A good cover letter should clearly demonstrate why you want the job at this particular bank and why you're suitable for it. It should provide a comprehensive and overall view of your life, your experience, and your humanity. And if there's no reason to utilize the cover letter to give additional context, then leave it short, to the point and typo-free. This part of your application doesn't need to add a lot of value, but it can be a deal breaker (no pun intended!) if it has poor grammar, poor formatting, or typos. Remember, a typo in the banking industry can be lethal and end up hurting a bank's reputation. Don't lose your chance at a job over a misspelled word.

Cover Letter Template

COVER LETTER TEMPLATE

Name
Mailing address
City, State Zip code
Professional E-mail Address ← [no nicknames or numbers]
Phone number

Date

Contact's name
Contact's title
Company name
Company mailing address

Dear Mr. or Ms. Last Name: ←[Avoid letters that start with "To Whom It May Concern"; being personal shows you've done your homework]

Start with a sentence that mentions what you're interested in contributing to [name of firm] through [name of position]. [This should show that you understand the broad goals of the firm and that you have a good grasp of how your role can advance these goals.] **Next, state why you are attracted to this bank (one or two sentences).** [Be specific. Bankers know that you are likely applying to all the big firms, so anything you can say that proves your special interest in this particular firm will earn you points. If you have been speaking to bankers at the firm, this is a great opportunity to mention them and your takeaways without just name-dropping.] **Finish with a sentence that lists the 2-3 attributes that make you a strong candidate for this position and a good fit for this company.** [Remember, the goal should always be to focus on skills you can contribute, not skills the position can contribute to you. I have seen too many candidates mention that banking will give them the best learning experience. While this may be true, it doesn't help me understand why I should invest in your learning over someone else's.]

In this paragraph, briefly provide evidence and examples to substantiate the skills you listed in the previous sentence. [Imagine that this paragraph represents the first minute of an interview. What would you say about yourself to catch a recruiter's attention? What have you done to prove your interest in banking? **If you need to explain any serious issues in your story, then this is the paragraph to do so.** Choose your words wisely so you don't sound like you're making excuses. Be professional, brief, and move on quickly to focus on the future and what you can bring to the job now.]

End by expressing your enthusiasm for an interview. Mention logistical points if there are any (e.g. your willingness to relocate). **Let them know that they should feel free to contact you for more information.** [This last paragraph is short and tends to be more of a formality. The safe route is to simply keep it that way, unless you have something brilliant to add that will sincerely convey your enthusiasm for this particular firm or job. Don't listen to career coaches who tell you to end with something aggressive like "I will contact you in two weeks." It doesn't change anything and sounds overly pushy.]

Sincerely,
Full name

X.

Investment Banking Recruitment

"They come looking, and once they have identified you as a strong candidate, they will take you out to a fancy dinner and open the floor up for you to show them how badly you want the internship."

The Recruiting Process

An internship is the best way to get a full-time offer, and attending a recruiting event is the best way to get an internship. Most banks only hire interns after their junior year of college, but some have programs for sophomores or even high school students. There is a good chance, if you are an exceptional intern that you could have a full-time offer plus a sign-on bonus by Thanksgiving. But if there isn't an offer in the wings from your internship, you need to be prepared to hit the ground sprinting come September. Have your resume, cover letters, and interview questions prepped. You have to be ready as early as possible to get an offer your senior year. Checking every company's career website for a listing of the special programs and the latest event calendar is key.

Once you've done all that, at long last, your interview with an investment banking recruiter has arrived. With it comes your shot at that summer internship that will hopefully transform into a full-time offer by the time it ends. You're confident that you will impress the recruiters, since you've been preparing for this day since you started college. You're calm, collected and ready to talk. But what to wear? How can you make yourself memorable?

Recruiters are sent out from major banks to the top 20 schools each year, trained to select only the brightest, sharpest, and most promising group of candidates from those schools. They come looking, and once they have identified you as a strong candidate, they will take you out to a fancy dinner and open the floor up for you to show them how badly you want the internship.

Have no fear whether they will remember you or not—they will. It's their job. After you meet them on the first day of a recruiting session, at the end of each day they go through their lists and digest your strong points, weak points, or things they really want to follow up with you about in an in-depth interview. They note all sorts of details that came up in your encounter, even concerns you may have raised. They want to give as many candidates as possible a chance to show them what they've got.

In recruiting sessions, it's extremely important that you make a solid and positive impression. Assuming you have done your research and you've networked, prepped, and practiced for the big day, your recruiting session should run smoothly. Between the session itself, and the few small touches for after the session is over, be sure to also remember the following:

- **You need to look sharp in professional business attire.**

    This would include a suit with a jacket for men, and a skirt or suit with a jacket for women. Bankers and the finance industry in general are very conservative. That means unusual hairstyles or an ungroomed look can make you look unprofessional and cost you points. Remember, this is a client servicing business so presentation matters.

- **You need to look credible, professional and mature.**

    This is because you need be able to represent the bank when dealing with older clients who expect a certain appearance. Leave the strong fragrances and bright colors at home and come wearing black, gray, or navy.

- **Send the recruiters a thank you email.**

    Speed is essential, so try to do this as soon as possible after an interview. Thank you notes create a one-on-one bond with the recruiter. It shows them that you understand the importance of following up, being courteous, and adding closure to your meeting. It also offers you one more chance to tell them, without a doubt, how badly you want the position.

    Investment banking values attention to detail, and a typo or wrong bank name in the subject line will kill your chances at this point in the game. Make sure you proofread your email several times before sending—including the email address it's being sent to!

Top Networking Techniques For Recruiting

You've heard it mentioned a dozen times before: you must network before you can even start thinking about a career in investment banking. People have told you to talk to banks, to go to lunch with employees, to forge relationships with alumni and to make sure there are reputable bankers that know you and can vouch for you. In investment banking, networking doesn't stop after you're offered a full-time job—if nothing else, it only increases. As your career continues, you may be offered a top-level management position based on the contacts and relationships you have built over the course of time. Networking is imperative in investment banking.

There are certain techniques to investment banking networking. At first, your networking should be more informal; reach out to people around your same age. Or, if you want to become an analyst, reach out to analysts, associates or even existing interns at the banks you're interested in. If you're an MBA student, reach out to associates, vice presidents or even analysts. Talking with an analyst about basic banking questions over lunch is probably better than discussing it with a vice president who may get the wrong impression about you. After you've made some initial contact with members of your network, review the points below to help you in your continued outreach.

- In addition to reaching out to people you don't know, you should also use **alumni information sessions** or recruiting events to network. These conversations you'll have there are where you show them that you're intelligent and professional; you also want to be able to chat about the recent news, financial impacts or other topics that you could bring up in a casual manner. When you're not engaged with an alumnus or recruiter, there is downtime where you should be **talking with your peers** and exchanging knowledge.

- You want to **create a buzz** about who you are and what you can offer a bank. But when it comes to networking, it is best to be natural about it and not overly aggressive. Much like dating, **you don't want to come on too strong,** but you do want to let them know you're interested and that you would like to spend some time getting to know more about them. If one analyst, associate, or intern cannot help you with questions, or doesn't have the time that month to have you come in and shadow them while they work, ask them if they can recommend anyone to you that could.

- It's important that you **build a contact list** that includes several people and banks that you're interested in. Stay consistent with your efforts without being overly pushy or persistent. You want to also learn as much about the industry as possible, so it's good to take this approach when you're **cold-calling a bank contact.** Be friendly and excited; see if you can set up a time to meet with them, talk about their job and spend an afternoon following them around. You will learn an insider's viewpoint which will be beneficial to your career.

Networking is an extremely helpful way to break into the business. When you combine your contact's positive reviews with your exceptional GPA, intriguing extracurricular activities, and strong financial knowledge, you are well on your way to landing a job with a bank. Networking can be a fun avenue; let it be an opportunity to talk with people while learning more about the industry and the job.

Question:

When networking over email, should I attach my resume?

Answer:

I highly encourage you to attach your resume to any initial email correspondence. You don't have to make a big deal about it and can simply write, "For your reference, attached is my resume." I used to have a hard time responding to emails from strangers when they did not include a resume. It was important for me to know who is the person behind this email, just like you already know to whom you're sending the email. If the student had a strong resume, I was also more apt to respond promptly. Your resume is your best way to show that you are worth someone's time and efforts, and that you've done your homework, have a typo-free and well-formatted resume, and good academics or work experience. There's also the possibility that the person may find something in common with you through your resume, like a shared interest, language, or a club they used to belong to when they were in college. This is precisely what networking is all about finding common grounds, so attaching your resume can potentially bring you a step closer. My advice is that you have nothing to lose, and you may in fact gain, by including it. So unless you know your resume does not highlight your abilities and would prefer using your personality rather than your credentials to network, then always attach your resume.

Insider Recruiting Advice

When it was recruiting season, I used to get a pile of over 100 resumes from one school alone. The team would schedule a conference call to narrow that pile down to about 12 to 25 candidates who would get invited to a first-round interview. The turnaround to make these invitations was usually just a few days. There is rarely any such thing as downtime in a banker's day, so you can imagine when they find the time to read every line on those 100 resumes . . . yes, you guessed it: never.

Instead, I used to start by pulling out all the resumes with names I recognized from students who had reached out to me in the past—some had even been in touch years before when they were just in their first year of college. This pile would naturally get special attention because I had already interacted with these candidates, knew more about their personality traits, and was sure that they were committed to banking since they had been so proactive. Unless someone had made a bad impression, appeared to lack personality, or generally had bad credentials (e.g. very low GPA), I would likely recommend these students to the committee.

Next, I would look at GPAs of the resumes left: the ones with really high GPAs got a second glance, a look through past work experience, and maybe a quick skim of the cover letter to fill any voids. (What I considered a high GPA varied by school, but it was typically a 3.5 to 3.7 or above.) The candidates who could complement their high GPA with leadership activities or strong work experience, especially in finance or a related field, were likely to make it on my list of nominees.

Of the resumes left with good GPAs, but not top ones (usually 3.2 to 3.5), I would add any with really strong work experience to my pile of "maybe's." Examples of strong work experience could be an internship with another investment bank (regardless of its size) or a finance/accounting position with a top company. Generally, anyone with experience at a bank or other Fortune 500 company got a second glance. These would be discussed with the committee only if we had more spots left to fill (often a couple of these might make it to the final list for an interview).

Then, I would take one last quick glance through the cover letters of the remaining pile to see if any of them spoke to me. If a candidate came across as particularly mature and professional, and displayed a strong connection to banking (through referencing other alumni they had spoken to or by showing initiative in some other way), then I would take a second glance at their resumes to see if they had a chance. In some cases, a candidate would also sincerely explain the reason for a weaker GPA or some other gap in their resume. If it sounded genuine or was a good reason, I would take a second look at the resume. Any cover letters with bad sentence structure, poor grammar, or typos would automatically disqualify that candidate. Sadly, when you're reviewing over 100 resumes, you have to take a harsh stance against poor preparation.

Once I had my pile of about 15 candidates, I still had to get on the phone with the other members of that school's recruiting team to compare my choices to theirs and select the final group. The students who were on each recruiter's list are invariably the ones who were proactive and had reached out to almost every team member prior to the recruiting season. These would immediately get an interview and usually took up almost half the slots, so the amount of spots left was limited. This is why networking is so important in this competitive field! It will truly pay off dividends for life.

When evaluating applications for full-time positions, we would sometimes run the list by students from that school who had just interned with us. They served as our insiders at the school and were expected to give candid feedback about their peers. We would even ask them questions like "If there was one person from your entire class that you would recommend, who would it be?" We would sometimes force them to select between two strong candidates to give us further insight into those candidates. Personally, I know that I landed my first-round interview at J.P. Morgan primarily because I had worked with many of the interns on school projects and they spoke favorably of my work ethic when approached by the recruiting team. It's important to remember that besides being your most accessible resource, your peers can also be your best advocates!

When I recruited at top undergraduate or business schools, the process was slightly different. We held so many events prior to the application deadline that we had usually compiled most of the list for first-round interviews before we ever got the resume pile from H.R. There are so many opportunities for students to network during recruiting season (information sessions, dinners, panel events, workshops, etc.) that we had a good sense of which students were truly interested in investment banking and our firm by the time applications were formally submitted.

I didn't have to spend a lot of time narrowing the pile of resumes to about 20 candidates. I usually had at least a dozen that I had grown to know quite well through the recruiting events. Other members of the recruiting team would have some overlap with my list but would also have their own top picks, so it was fairly easy to fill the slots. There were little to no spots left for students who failed to show up at these events or didn't contact us in some way ahead of the deadline.

Question:

I tried reaching out to a recruiter I met at a conference, but I never heard back. Should I try contacting them again or is that inappropriate?

Answer:

Don't be afraid to reach out more than twice if you don't hear back from a recruiter or alumnus within two weeks. Most people do not mind being contacted more than once and can always choose to ignore you again the second time. From my experience, the reason for not getting a response usually means you caught someone at a busy time. Politely reaching out again often pays off. If you tried a phone call the first time, then try an email the second time.

Even when I got emails from candidates who would probably not be a good fit for the job, I always responded. Sometimes, I didn't respond, but it would be for one of the following reasons:

- *The email was too long. Bankers are trained to be perfectionists, so if an email required a lengthier response, I would vow to set aside time to write a detailed response in the future. Somehow, that extra time never gets set aside, so the task just keeps getting pushed off until it never ends up happening. Lesson: keep your correspondences short and your asks simple. Do not ask long questions that are better answered over a phone call; instead, ask for the phone call and mention briefly what you'd like to discuss, so the person knows what they're committing to.*

- *I received the email or phone call at a busy time or while I was traveling. This is a classic example of an email that simply slipped through the cracks. People have a hard time saying no to eager students who come across as mature, so use this to your advantage and ask again. In a worse case scenario, the person will ignore you again or will say no to answering your questions. Both of those can help you plan your next course of action.*

XI

The Investment Banking Interview

"The most important part of your interview is correctly conveying your story. While you may not get the exact question that you prepped for, you may find that your prepared answers are still relevant to other questions."

Interview Prep Work and Analysis

There's nothing that combines stress and excitement like a really important interview. You're thrilled about the possibility of getting a job or internship out of the deal, and you're also stressed that you're not going to be ready in time to really stand out and own the day. When prepping for an investment banking interview, you need to be memorable, sharp as a tack, personable and able to demonstrate that you're the right match for the position they are seeking.

Anyone about to undergo an important interview would love a sneak peek at the interviewer's list of questions. Preparing for all the possible questions can be frustrating, confusing, and exhausting—especially when you will most likely only have a dozen questions in a 30 to 45 minute interview. I can remember being extremely frustrated spending long nights prepping specific answers to questions I might never get! But trust me, it's not all for nothing. Preparing for the questions actually helps guide you indirectly as you piece together "your story."

Remember, it's the journey you take in preparing that's important, not the destination. Someone once told me that no matter what happens as a result of applying to investment banking, you will learn a lot about finance, business, and yourself throughout the preparation process. It's absolutely true! If you can approach your preparation phase with this attitude, that you're bound to gain something valuable in life regardless of the outcome, then the preparation will be much more enjoyable.

There are a few ways, in addition to question prep, that you can make yourself memorable:

- If you're at a recruiting session, **wear a name tag**. Introduce yourself at the beginning of a conversation, and remind them of your name when you thank them on your way out.

- **Ask smart questions** that show you're ahead of your peers because you've done your research. It also helps to show them that you're picky, and not completely desperate for the opportunity. It's a little like playing hard to get. Be confident in your delivery and make them show you why you may be a good fit for their bank.

- In your interview, recruiters are more than willing to let you **take the floor**, but you had better know how to direct the interview—or you could spend the whole time chatting about the final inning of the baseball game instead of why you want the job.

- When it's time to ask them questions, you should **avoid generic questions about banking and try to ask targeted ones**, like "What has been your favorite deal to work on recently?" or "What attracted you to your group?" or "What are some changes the bank is currently experiencing that have bankers talking?"

- It's smart to **ask questions that span various categories**. Ask one about the firm or group, another about thoughts on a popular deal, or one about the culture of the bank. Make sure that the questions are ones that the interviewer will be excited to talk about. If you ask about a deal or topic that they know nothing about, you will make them feel uncomfortable and it will be unpleasant for everyone involved!

- It helps **demonstrate your knowledge on the industry** when you can intelligently speak about a deal that's going on in the market. This will let them know that you're committed to banking, are genuinely interested in the work, and have been proactive in your preparation.

Four Things to Know Before Your Interview

1. **Nix "hard worker syndrome."**

Your interview should not be a thirty minute session of you repeating "I am a hard worker. Did I mention I'm a hard worker? . . ." over and over again. If when they ask you, "why investment banking," you say, "well, I'm hard-worker, I really like the fast-paced environment and I really love numbers," don't respond "well, I really like numbers and I'm a hard-worker," to "why should we choose you over another candidate?" You've just wasted the second opportunity to add something to your candidacy by repeating the same response.

To avoid repetition, make a list on the left side of a page of the questions you expect to receive (see the list of "Always Asked" and "Commonly Asked" questions as a reference). These should include: why investment banking, why you, why now, what are some of your flaws and qualities, why did you choose your school, former internship, and major, and extracurricular activities. Then, on the right side of the page, create a bulleted list of points you want to make during your interview. These can be personality traits, past achievements, examples of times when you took initiative, etc.

Now that you have the two lists, start answering the questions on the left using the points listed on the right. Ideally, you only want to use each point once. One or two of them might be worth reiterating, but generally an interviewer will remember everything you say so there is no reason to be repetitive. This exercise will help to ensure that you don't repeat yourself. It will also force you to find an opportunity to share every important point in your application during the interview. When you walk out of the meeting, the worst feeling is to think, "Oh! I forgot to say . . . and now I probably won't get the job because of that!"

If one of the questions on your list doesn't get asked, don't panic. Your goal is to not leave that room without conveying all of your qualifications. When they ask you, "Do you have any questions for us?" You can say, "In my last internship, I did a, b, and c, and really enjoyed all three. In this position, how is one's time split between the three tasks?" You have just gotten one of your points across while also asking a relevant question to help you decide if this is the right place for you—sometimes, the best place to get any outstanding points across can be when it's your turn to ask questions!

2. **Be Honest**.

If you're asked a technical question and you absolutely don't know the answer, then starting to answer that question is not a good idea—you will just dig yourself a hole. Bankers like to probe, and they will keep probing until you hit a wall. A mature candidate would stop at some point and say, "I don't actually know the answer to that question. Can I get back to you?"

There are some questions that recruiters will expect candidates to know, even if they haven't studied finance. These include basic banking topics like the various valuation techniques or the accounting of how the three statements are connected. They will also ask other, more difficult technical questions to test your knowledge further. If you pretend you know the answer when you don't, you will simply make yourself look bad and ruin the good rapport you had built during the interview until that point.

When I recruited, we were specifically instructed to ask follow-up questions and probe every response, whether it was a technical or behavioral question. Know that this will definitely happen in your interviews. The worst thing you can do in this situation is to make up responses when you're unsure. Avoid the embarrassment of getting caught; be honest and sincere when in doubt.

3. **Avoid the Chatty Kathy**.

Some bankers will try to chat you up to test your ability to get down to business: they will waste a lot of time talking about the weather or the sports game last night, when what you need to do is show them why you're fit for the job. If you waste 15 minutes in a 30 minute interview, it might make you more likable, but when that recruiter has to go in front of the recruiting committee and vouch for you, they won't have much to present.

Young interviewers often think it's a good sign when they're having casual banter with an interviewer. Be careful not to get too comfortable. This is still an evaluation by a more senior person and is meant to be your only chance to discuss your qualifications. Spend a few minutes getting to know each other, then cut straight to the chase and start with the questions. Don't assume it's entirely out of your control. Take a few minutes to chat about whatever, then signal a change by asking, "What questions can I answer for you today?" Remember, the more questions you can answer in that half hour slot, the more chances you've given yourself to get the job.

4. **Good Cop, Bad Cop**.

It's quite common to be interviewed by two people. First, don't get nervous with two sets of eyes staring at you intently. Second, know how to feed off of these dynamics—don't give one person more attention than the other because they appear to be nicer. Respect both individuals equally and show them that you're not fazed by the old "good cop, bad cop" trick. You're confident, you want this job, and you're the right candidate for it.

There are times when an interview goes completely wrong and you know leaving it that you're probably not going to get the offer. In these situations, there is a chance that the interviewer will offer you feedback that tells you how you could improve in future interviews. Use this information to your benefit. But be careful that you don't take their advice too seriously and go overboard on your next interview.

After my first round, the recruiter was kind enough to give me valuable feedback in preparation for my superday. He suggested that I be a bit more aggressive and show how badly I want the job . . . I ended up being so aggressive during my superday that I later found out one interviewer was jokingly scared of not giving me the job!

Six Things to Avoid in an Interview

1. **No Bullshit.**

Bankers can smell it a mile away. Avoid saying nice things to get what you want. Keep it real. Bankers appreciate it when you are straight to the point and efficient. It's a business where the hours are long so they are especially aggressive about not wasting time.

2. **Don't Be Wishy-Washy.**

Sometimes, you can get tripped up when the interviewer suggests that you may be better equipped to work in a different department of the bank, or in another job altogether like consulting. This is a trick question! Don't be polite and tell them it's a good idea, that you will look into it. When they ask what you would do if you don't get into banking, say you will keep trying.

3. **Don't Avoid Difficult Questions.**

There may be holes in your experience or a downslide in your academic work: this is no reason to sugarcoat your answer or try to pass over it with a general response. They will keep trying to figure out the real answer during the interview. Be honest about why you didn't do certain things. Share your real reasons why you've done what you've done. Again, appealing to a recruiter's human side by being sincere can go a long way.

4. **Don't Be Too Quick To Answer.**

Try not to answer too early and prematurely on the technical questions. Take the time to say, "Let me take a quick minute to think about this correctly." You can write things down and ask for a little more information if needed. Giving the right answer a minute later is much more valuable than giving the wrong one right away.

5. **Don't Pretend That You're Smarter Than You Are.**

On any question that you're unsure about, it's okay to say "I don't know about this, but I can get back to you." It shows you're proactive. Then get back to them as soon as the interview ends!

6. **Don't Ramble.**

It's easy to get talking about something when you're nervous, and then carry on and on. A banker will let you take the floor and speak, so make sure you take control of the interview *and* take notice when you've answered the question. Instead of rambling, stop yourself after a minute or two, once you feel you've answered it sufficiently, and say "does that answer your question?" They will ask you for more information if needed. Remember, it's a dialogue you're creating in an interview, not a one-way street.

Non-Technical and Frequently Asked Questions

Prepare to answer a list of specific questions that almost every interviewer will ask. Questions like these will take up over half the interview and preparing for them will ensure you nail this portion of the interview. Be sure to run your responses by mentors and advisers for advice and feedback before the interview.

The most important part of your interview is to correctly convey your story and give memorable examples to back it up. While you may not get the exact question that you prepped for, you may find that your prepared answers are still relevant to other questions. The long list of questions you prepare forces you to think about things you've probably never thought of before or things you haven't thought of in a long time. This may include why you made certain choices in life or how you reacted in certain situations. Critical thinking like this helps your interviews.

Always Asked

1. Tell us about yourself or "Walk me through your resume."

2. What is investment banking?

3. Why do you want to work in investment banking?

4. What is the role of an analyst/associate?

5. Why are you interested in this firm?

6. Why should we choose you?

7. Why did you choose the university you're enrolled at?

8. What do you consider your greatest qualities?

9. Where do you see yourself in the future?

10. Do you have any questions for us?

11. Are you applying anywhere else?

Commonly Asked

1. Tell us about a banking deal that you like.

2. Which extracurricular activity do you enjoy the most? Why?

3. Describe a teamwork experience.

4. What would your teammates say about you?

5. What is one thing your teammates would ask you to improve on?

6. What job would you pursue if you don't get a job in investment banking? (**Note: trick question!** Answer should still be Investment Banking.)

7. Describe how you envision your first day on the job.

8. Are you interested in any specific groups, and why?

Possible Questions (varies by interviewer, and more likely to appear in second rounds):

1. Describe a negative teamwork experience and how the situation was resolved.

2. Tell me about a time when you had to complete a deliverable under a tight deadline and how you dealt with the situation.

3. How do you choose your friends?

4. How was your relationship with your boss in your former internship or work experience?

5. In your last feedback session with your former boss, what were some of the qualities highlighted? What were some areas for improvement?

6. What do you think are the best qualities for building strong client relationships?

7. What is something you are passionate about? Why?

8. Tell me about a time when you needed to provide criticism or difficult feedback to

someone.

9. Tell me about a time when you were on the receiving end of difficult feedback. How did you respond?

10. What do you think was the role of bankers in the mortgage crisis?

11. Imagine that you find a mistake in the numbers just 10 minutes before an important client meeting, how you would handle the situation?

12. What do you think differentiates this firm from others?

Technical Interview Questions

The right answers to technical questions will be learned on the job, so don't stress about needing to know all the details for a perfect response. The interview is simply meant to show that you have given them *some* thought and that you are not illogical in your thought process.

You are also demonstrating how interested you are in these topics. Your goal here is to have the right answer to the most basic technical questions and a *sense* of the right answer to the others. Again, it can be extremely helpful to run your responses by a peer or a professor prior to the interview.

Finance & Valuation:

1. What are the various valuation methods?

2. How would you value a public company?

3. How would you value a private company?

4. How would you value a local pizza shop?

5. How would you value a painting?

6. How would you value a vineyard?

7. How would you value a company that has yet to generate any revenue?

8. When would you choose one valuation technique over another?

9. How do you account for net operating losses (NOL's) when valuing a company?

10. What are examples of events that make trading comparables volatile in the short term?

11. Why does the value of a DCF differ from a company's trading value?

12. Are trading/public comparable multiples typically greater or lesser than transaction

transaction value)?

34. What is the right numerator (enterprise value or equity value) for an EPS multiple? A revenue multiple? An EBIT or EBITDA multiple? Unlevered cash flow multiple?

35. When would you use a revenue multiple over an EBITDA multiple?

36. When would you use an EBITDA multiple over an EPS multiple?

37. What are the advantages and disadvantages of using EBITDA as a metric to compare companies?

38. How do you calculate EPS?

39. How do Research and Development expenses (R&D) affect an EBITDA multiple?

40. What happens to a company's P/E multiple if it acquires a company with a lower P/E multiple?

41. Walk me through the treasury stock method. Why do companies use it?

42. What is preferred stock?

43. Why do companies issue dividends?

44. What time of companies don't issue dividends?

45. If you were thinking of buying stock in a company, how would you go about determining the value of a share?

46. How do you determine the return on a stock?

47. In a scenario where a company has a lot of cash on their balance sheet, what would you advise it to do?

48. What are the different methods a company can employ to raise cash?

49. When should a company issue stock to raise cash?

50. When should a company use debt to raise cash?

51. Compare the pros and cons of using stock vs. debt to raise cash?

52. Describe the benefits of liquidity for a company.

53. What can a company do to increase its liquidity?

54. Discuss the various financial ratios useful to assess a company's performance.

55. What are examples of multiples used for measuring credit worthiness?

56. What are ways to determine the optimal debt level (i.e. leverage) of a company?

57. What is the debt capacity of a target when it has EBITDA of $50 million and a 5.0x leverage ratio?

58. What is a leveraged buyout (LBO)?

59. In an LBO, what is the maximum purchase price that a financial sponsor can offer for a target with EBITDA of $50 million, a 5.0x leverage ratio, and assuming a 25% equity contribution?

60. How would you value a bond?

61. What is the Net Present Value (NPV) of a $1,000 cash flow in perpetuity if it is discounted at 10%?

62. What are the different types of bonds that a company can issue?

63. What is the difference between senior and subordinated debt?

64. What is the difference between secured and unsecured debt?

65. What happens to debt and equity holders when a company files for bankruptcy?

66. If a company sells a division for $100 million, what is the impact on the value of the company?

67. Why would a company choose to break up its divisions into separate companies?

68. What is a Sum-of-the-Parts analysis and when is it beneficial to use?

69. What happens to a company's stock price when it announces an acquisition?

70. What happens to a company's stock price when it announces that it has been acquired?

71. What can a company do to avoid a hostile takeover?

72. How does a poison pill work?

73. When would a company use a poison pill?

74. Explain what is meant when a merger is considered dilutive vs. accretive.

75. Describe the differing dynamics of advising a potential buyer vs. a seller in an M&A transaction.

76. What are some reasons why two seemingly unrelated companies might choose to merge?

77. What are some of the biggest reasons that cause mergers to fail in the long-term?

78. Besides the results of a valuation analysis, what are some of the other considerations that would drive a buyer's offer bid?

Economy:

1. What are current trends in Investment Banking?

2. What is the S&P 500 trading at?

3. What is the Dow Jones Industrial Average trading at?

4. What is the price of a barrel of oil?

5. What are the rates of a 30-day, 1-year, 5-year, and 10-year treasury note?

6. Discuss how the Federal Reserve's approach to interest rates has impacted the U.S. and global economy in the past year?

7. What is LIBOR?

8. How does the yield curve work?

Accounting:

1. Walk me through each of the three financial statements.

2. How are the three financial statements related?

3. Which of the three statements is most important for valuing a company?

4. Which of the three statements is most important for analyzing a company's performance?

5. If you could only use one line on a financial statement to value a company, which one would you use and how?

6. How do you calculate operating cash flow?

7. What is Working Capital? How do you calculate it?

8. In the cash flow statement, in what section would you classify a stock repurchase?

9. In the cash flow statement, in what section would you classify cash collected from accounts receivables?

10. In the cash flow statement, in what section would you classify depreciation? (**Note**: **Trick Question!**)

11. In the cash flow statement, in what section would you classify an issuance of debt?

12. In the cash flow statement, in what section would you classify a purchase of equipment?

13. If Accounts Receivables decreased, what is the impact to Working Capital?

14. What is the difference between operating and capital leases?

15. How would you record the purchase of land?

16. How would you record the purchase of machinery?

17. How does the sale of machinery affect the three statements?

18. What are examples of deferred liabilities?

19. What are examples of deferred assets?

20. What is goodwill?

21. What is accrual based accounting?

22. How do you account for options?

23. What is the difference between liabilities and expenses?

24. When do you record revenue?

25. What is operating profit?

26. If a company purchases a piece of machinery for $1000 that depreciates over the next 10 years, walk me through the impact on each of the financial statements by the end of year one.

27. How does a change in D&A impact EBITDA? (**Note: Trick Question!**)

28. Describe LIFO and FIFO for inventory accounting.

29. What is the impact on the financial statements from using LIFO vs. FIFO?

30. What is convertible debt and how do you account for it?

31. Describe purchase accounting and how a company's statements change when it acquires another company?

32. When do you use the various methods of accounting (market value, equity, and consolidated) to report investments in other companies?

33. What is a tax shield?

The Toughest Question: Identifying Your Weaknesses

Standing before the banking tribunal, pull out all stops and show them who you really are. Don't sugarcoat yourself to be some super-human wonder banker; instead, bring to the table a package that showcases your greatest assets and skills, previous achievements, and that you were born to do this job.

It's also a good idea to fully understand what weaknesses you have and to acknowledge some of them when they are asked of you. You do not want to give them a general answer, like "My biggest weakness is that I work too hard." Really? Well, that's not really a weakness in this job scenario: it is a strength, and the interviewer is not going to be satisfied with your answer. Dig deep, be honest, and try not to shoot yourself in the foot by answering your biggest weakness with a trait that you really should not have. For example, you wouldn't want to tell the interviewer that your biggest weakness is you're super-competitive or you have a hard time trusting teammates.

Unfortunately, there is no right answer that I can share with you to the weakness question; only wrong answers. I have only encountered this question once in my interviews and have never asked it when I recruited, but I've heard horror stories from many peers who lost the job because of a poor answer. Ideally, you want to mention a weakness that caused a failure or setback in your life, but from which you have recently grown. Acknowledging a failure shows maturity, and sharing your lesson learned demonstrates that this is no longer anything for the interviewer to be concerned with. If you give a thoughtful and honest response, you should be in the clear.

In response to the question, I once said that I don't usually take the time to enjoy or relish in the aftermath of a big accomplishment, such as completing a difficult project. I often dive right into the next project without taking a break or setting aside time to celebrate the achievement. Consequently, I have noticed myself burning out too soon when working on my next project. To rectify this, I said that I now force myself to take some downtime in between big projects to ensure that I am giving my all to the next challenge, rather than starting on the wrong foot with the little steam I have left in me. Since it was clear from looking at my record that I was a hard-worker, the interviewer didn't take this to mean that I burned out because I was a weak performer. Rather, it came across as someone who noticed a valid weakness and resolved it. The interviewer didn't dwell on my response, which is exactly the reaction you want for this type of a question. A bad reaction would entail a lot of follow-up questions that probe deeper into your weakness and attempt to find loopholes in your story.

Show them that you have heart and that you are sincere, honest, and excited to start in your new career field. Open the door to your story and let them take a look around and get to know you. Crack a crevice into your brain and show off your stunning management and finance skills. Prove you were born to do the job and the rest will follow.

XII

Manage Your Banking Expectations

"On a bad day, you most likely have made dinner plans with a friend . . . [but] as the day is coming to a close, a deal explodes and you end up staying and working well past dinner until 2 a.m."

Change Your Banking Expectations

The buzz of Wall Street. Early morning commuters bustling through the packed streets of Manhattan and pouring out of subway tunnels. They have coffee in hand and *The Wall Street Journal* tucked under an arm. When you think of a day in the life of an investment banker, images from a movie may play in your mind . . . but reality rarely resembles Hollywood's depictions.

Like any career field, there are good days and there are bad days. As an investment banker, a good day includes smooth transactions, deals running as scheduled, and meetings with the client or a board. These days could also involve interactions with world business leaders—the people that run top Fortune 500 companies. A good day could also feature one of the deals you're working announced and appearing in the media. But it's the bad days that sneak up on you. If you don't wake up with any precursor signs of a bad day, like stubbing your toe out the door, spilling food on your collared shirt during lunch, or finding out at 3 a.m. that something has gone wrong with a deal, your bad days usually start out like any other. In fact, on a bad day you most likely have made dinner plans with a friend, thinking, "All the deals I'm on are under control and I should be able to get out early enough for dinner." As the day is coming to a close, a deal explodes and you end up staying and working well past dinner until 2 a.m." Unfortunately, working in an ever-changing landscape, these days happen fairly often.

Some groups are more unpredictable than others. Product groups that work on live transactions tend to be a little more volatile. When you are working on live deals, it doesn't matter what you've got going on in your personal life: you have a client on the other end of the deal that you have to satisfy. Other groups, like coverage groups or those that follow the markets, may have more time and space to work on their deals. Market-following groups work hardest during the day when the market is active. Usually, they can go home and start again earlier in the morning. But most groups in investment banking don't have that luxury and can be working until any hour of the night.

Every bank has its own proven culture and that's largely driven by the managing directors in those groups and the group head. So you might see some groups, for instance, offer the bankers one guaranteed weekend a month that they'll have off. That comes directly from the group head noticing that his or her team needs a little break and instituting those policies—it's not by industry focus, it's by bank and by group.

Chain Of Command

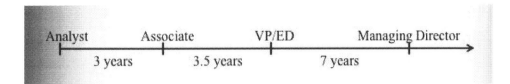

When you start out on your investment banking journey, most people don't get past the idea of the thrilling life they are going to lead and the money they are going to make. They don't always take into consideration the work itself and the home you can make for yourself in the long run if you manage your career proactively. In order to understand how you climb the ladder, you need to know the hierarchy of the bank.

- On the base level, there are **interns**. Often, interns are made first-year bankers the following summer if they excelled during their internships.

- First-year **analysts** are usually fresh out of college and undergo a six to eight week training program before they start working.

- The first-year bankers are signed full-time for two years. If they are exceptional at their job, they will be invited to stay on with the bank for another year. During that rigorous third year, they will be tested on their ability to handle the responsibilities of an **associate**. A handful of them will succeed and be promoted. The more common way to become an associate is to be recruited from an MBA or JD program.

- After at least seven years in, as both an analyst and an associate, you can be promoted to **vice president**. If you continue to do impeccable work by generating revenues, creating and maintaining strong client relationships, and bringing in deals, you can be promoted to **executive director** (or "director", "associate director", or "senior VP") after about three or four years.

- If you continue to climb, you can eventually reach the highest point in banking—the **managing director** or managing partner. At this point, you can also become the **head of a group**.

An investment banking career can change your life—and it can also make you wish you had more of a life outside of it. At the end of a grueling day of hard work, long hours and stress, keep in mind this is a job you earned, and you deserve to enjoy the fruits of your labor. Remember to treat yourself as well as you treat your clients!

Salary and Perks

Estimated Salaries

The banking industry is typically hush-hush about salaries and benefits, but here are the latest estimates for employees:

- **Analyst Internship Salary**: About $1,500/week for 10 weeks

- **Associate Internship Salary**: About $2,500/week for 10 weeks

- **Analyst Salary:**

  - Sign-on bonus of about $10,000

  - Base salary: $70,000 to $90,000 (1st to 3rd year analyst)

  - **Top bonus**: $70,000 to $100,000 based on performance (1st to 3rd year analyst).

  - Note: Analyst bonuses can vary greatly from year to year depending on the firm's performance.

- **Associate Salary:**

  - $40,000 sign-on (for analysts who were promoted)

  - Salary: $125,000 to $175,000 (1st to 3rd year associate)

  - $40,000 "stub" bonus (first six months of being an associate)

  - **Top bonus**: $100,000 to $175,000 (might be partially paid in stock).

  - Note: Associate bonuses can vary greatly from year to year depending on the firm and group's performance.

Benefits for analysts and associates are fairly standard:

- Good medical, prescription, vision, and dental plans

- A 401k retirement savings account (Most banks will also match your 401k contribution up to a certain percentage amount.)

- Sick leave

- Two to four weeks of paid vacation

People who want to become bankers have to be aware that they will not be able to trade stocks easily because of the many conflicts of interest. Any stock investment will need to be pre-approved by the Group Head. Exiting a stock requires a month notice in advance, so I've known bankers who had to watch their stock investments crash while not being able to do anything to get out of them. Instead, you can invest in mutual funds—just not as easily in individual stocks.

Other perks that might be of interest and vary by bank include:

- On-site gym for fitness

- Discounts on the bank's financial services, such as checking accounts or brokerage accounts,

- Discounts on museums, hotels, phone plans, and many other retail products

- Daily dinner allowance of around $25

Vacation Days

Whether you will get to use all your vacation days will depend largely on the culture in your group, and your ability to manage your time off. If you let deal teams cancel your vacations easily—or even worse, if you don't actually ask for time off—then you will likely not use up your full amount of paid vacation. Most banks have a rule that you have to take seven consecutive days off at some point during the year, so they try to help you manage this.

I used to strive to take a week off around Christmas and New Year's. Most bankers and clients will be out of the office during that time, so this was fairly easy. But there was one year when I had to come back to work immediately after Christmas to work on a deal. I was a third year analyst and had essentially began serving as an associate; I even had to be on the phone with my Managing Director on my way to Christmas Eve dinner because one of our clients had an issue that we had to resolve. Try explaining that to your family!

I also took two days off sometime in March or April and usually went away on a five day weekend somewhere warm. You have to remember: weekends almost count as weekdays, so you have to ask for weekends off too, even though they don't technically count toward your vacation allowance! In August, I would try to take 10 days off to go away on a long trip somewhere exotic and treat myself to a nice hotel with a relaxing spa. August is a quiet month in general because most executives are on vacation, so this was always a good time to sneak out.

In my four years of banking, I was able to use up almost all my vacation time, but that required a lot of advance planning with my deal teams and leaving things in order during my absence. It also helps if you request time off during fairly slow times of the year, like the Holidays or August. Making the time to schedule a little break every few months will keep you motivated and energized.

XIII.

A Day In the Life

"You may wake up thinking you have a good idea of the day that lies ahead, but you will be wrong most of the time—and this doesn't change with seniority!"

A Real Day in the Life of an Investment Banker

There is no "typical" day for bankers. That's one of the qualities of the job that makes it so exciting. You may wake up thinking you have a good idea of the day that lies ahead, but you will be wrong most of the time—and this doesn't change with seniority! No two projects have the same deal dynamics. Every deal will have different team members, different clients, and different market tensions, that all need to be managed in their own way. If you like unpredictability and being challenged by new tasks every day, then you will likely enjoy the hectic day of an investment banker.

I was once on my way cross-country to meet a potential buyer and facilitate a site visit of a company we were selling. When I landed, I checked my emails and discovered that the employees of the factory had just gone on strike and would be picketing on our drive into the site! I had to immediately get on the phone with my team and agree on the right way to manage the situation. The strike set our deal back by a few months. While that kind of unpredictability is unusual, it goes to demonstrate how easily your day (or your next few months!) can quickly change.

On average, you can expect to work at least a dozen hours a day on weekdays, and likely a little less on weekends. You will often get to start later on weekends—maybe around noon and leave in time to catch dinner or a night out. But there will also be a few weekends in a row when it won't feel like a weekend at all. I've had many times when I thought my Saturday would be okay, only to be woken up early on Saturday morning with an unexpected call about something we need to finish by Monday. Being called in to work at 10am on a Saturday is something that most of your friends will not understand, but that's how you make the big bucks—and fortunately you'll get to order a big brunch from Seamless to help wake you up.

There will be nights when you can leave at 8 p.m. and other nights when you won't leave until 3 a.m. or 4 a.m. a few days in a row. This goes equally for both analysts and associates. When I used to get my work done early, it was such a treat. I would practically be bouncing with joy on my way home and felt like the world was my oyster! There were times when it felt like I had been working non-stop for months, but suddenly a deal would "die"—a term we use in banking to describe deals that have been canceled—and my weekend would unexpectedly become free.

Since I had been working so hard, I would check in with my staffer (the person who assigns projects) to confirm that I could go out of town for the weekend and then would jump a flight to visit my family or take the 3-hour non-stop trip to the Bahamas with a partner-in-crime. Being adventurous and learning to take things as they come makes banking a much more enjoyable profession!

In the next section you'll see an "average" day in the life of an analyst and associate, meant to give you an idea of the work process on a daily basis. On "non-average" days, you might get to attend an intimate client meeting and hear a CEO discuss his vision for a famous brand; listen to a Board make a monumental decision for a company; announce a deal and watch the market react on one of the many TVs throughout the building; or take a long celebratory lunch with a Managing Director at a fancy restaurant (his or her treat of course!). Days like those are the ones that make the job particularly satisfying, and they happen often enough to keep you motivated.

A Day in the Life of an Analyst

7:30 a.m.: You wonder what that annoying loud noise is in your dream, then realize it's your alarm, wake up and slap it angrily to shut it off. If you're a snoozer like me, you might need to set it a bit earlier to ensure you're actually up by 7:30 a.m.! The first thing you'll do is check your Blackberry to know what awaits you at the office. You may have to answer a few emails quickly for the senior team members that have been up since 6:00 a.m., which is only a few hours after you went to sleep!

Most of the time, there will be some unsettling email that will have you thinking of all the possible work scenarios during your shower. If you're disciplined, you'll learn to avoid the Blackberry as soon as you wake up, and look at it only on your way to work. Your commute to work could be an eight minute walk, or a longer subway ride—either way, you're likely to always feel a little late since there is no official start time for work.

9:00 a.m.: Start of your day in the office. If you had a long night and you're a more senior analyst, you might get to come in at 9:30 or even at 10:00 a.m. if you don't have a call or meeting scheduled.

9:30 a.m.: You've had a quick breakfast at your desk. You put on your headset and get ready for today's first conference call. As a first-year analyst, you will most likely listen and take notes. The call could be to update a client, to discuss project deliverables with your deal team, to answer questions of potential buyers about a business you're selling, to negotiate a contract with lawyers, and so on. As these various parties get to know you, you will begin to interact more directly with them.

10:30 a.m.: Respond to emails. Think of next steps coming out of the conference call. They may require you to make changes to a model or PowerPoint presentation, contact other parties to schedule follow-ups, update a tracking sheet, etc.

11:30 a.m.: Meet with an associate on one of your deals to discuss changes that you have to make to an analysis this afternoon.

12:30 p.m.: Pick up lunch with a few colleagues from the neighborhood or the cafeteria and eat at your desk while reviewing emails, reading equity research reports for a company you're valuing, or looking through a PowerPoint presentation you're working on.

Occasionally, you won't have any immediate deadlines and can enjoy a quick lunch with friends outside the office or in a conference room. There are sometimes group lunches organized to introduce you to a Managing Director or to celebrate a milestone.

2:00 p.m.: Your food coma starts to set in and you find it very difficult to concentrate. You send messages like "Zzzzzz" to your friend in another group (in my case, my roommate Lauren) and hope that they enlighten you with a brilliant way to wake up. Instead, you resort to a quick cup of coffee/tea from the pantry or a chocolate bar from the vending machine to give you some much-needed energy, and you get back to work.

3:00 p.m.: You may have another call or a meeting with bankers from other groups that are working on a deal with you. You listen while senior team members discuss next steps and update you on calls they've had with clients or other external parties. At some point, once everyone has agreed on what needs to be done, they will all turn to you and confirm that you got it. This is the dreaded moment for an analyst because all the work flows downward, so the brunt of the work falls on your shoulders! You might ask a few clarifying questions or discuss the limits of the model that will prevent you from completing the analysis they desire, but eventually you'll agree on what needs to get done, go back to your desk and get cranking.

4:00 p.m.: Time to work as fast as you can so that you can salvage your night and get some sleep. You might call the research group to get them started on pulling some of the analyses you need, or you might submit some slides to get formatted and printed from the presentation staff. Learning to delegate can become your best asset to producing high-quality, efficient work.

5:15 p.m.: You put some music on your headset and work on the spreadsheets that need to be changed. You check the resulting numbers regularly to make sure that you haven't made a mistake. Once you make a mistake in the model, it becomes very difficult to find, so you check often and save new versions of the file each time!

7:30 p.m.: You're proud of the work you've completed in the last few hours and get ready to order dinner. Most banks will give you an allowance for approximately $25 each night. You crowd around one person's desk to order food—there are hundreds of restaurants in New York to choose from. You can order alone too, but it's more fun to eat with others and only one person will have to go downstairs to pick up the delivery when the food arrives. $25 gets you a nice dinner, with a starter or dessert.

8:15 p.m.: You submit your latest work to the associate on your team. You run down to the lobby to pick up your dinner and eat in a conference room with everyone else. Some rooms might even have big screen TVs for you to take your mind off work for a bit. If you're trying to get out of the office early, you might choose to eat at your desk while you work or skip ordering altogether so you can eat out. However, you will most likely eat at the office every day except maybe Fridays or weekends.

8:45 p.m.: You meet with your associate to discuss your work and what still needs to get done today.

9:00 p.m.: You get back to your desk and incorporate any documents you may have received from the research or presentation groups on another transaction you're executing and send out the latest work to that deal team. Then, you begin to process the changes from the earlier work you submitted to your associate.

Midnight: You're done processing the associate's changes. You email the revised draft to your entire deal team, including the Managing Director or client's CFO this time. The associate may want to take one last look before you hit send. You drop off a printed copy on the Managing Director's chair. Depending on the number of changes you had to make, you could be done an hour or two earlier, or even hours later. The time when you finally get to go home will also depend on whether you have things to do on other projects, or whether the work can wait to be completed the following day. As you prove yourself and build a strong reputation for dependability in your first year, your deal teams will begin to trust that you will produce high quality work with minimal errors by the necessary deadline. This will allow you to control your schedule a bit better and leave some work to be completed the next morning.

12:30 a.m.: You get home, take a quick shower, and rush over to the neighborhood bar to meet your roommate or an old college friend. The beauty of investment banking is that the job is usually located in some of the world's greatest cities with plenty to do late into the night, every night! If you're exhausted or have a particularly stressful start the next day, you go home to unwind with a movie and call it a night. This is when having the right roommate who shares your lifestyle can make a huge difference!

I have found that **the best bankers are the ones who lead full social lives outside of work.** It's a job that gives you the money to make the most of the little free time you get, and those who take advantage of this seem to be among the stronger performers. On my year-end performance reviews, I was always commended on my work attitude and the positive impact I had on the group's culture. I have no doubt that this was a direct result of the fun that I had outside of work; it helped me tackle each day with a smile rather than a tired frown.

A Day in the Life of an Associate

7:00 a.m.: Wake up a little earlier than the analyst, because you need to be in the office to answer questions from senior team members and the client—those individuals will start firing questions at you bright and early! The good news is you probably got a little more sleep than the analyst. One way to view the partnership between junior team members is that the analyst takes the night shift while the associate covers the morning shift. Their days will overlap for the most part, but one will stay a little longer (sometimes a lot) and the other will start a little earlier to manage the morning work flow.

8:00 a.m.: If you had a late work night and no morning meetings, you might be able to come in later. You grab a quick breakfast at your desk and get ready for your first meeting.

9:00 a.m.: You get on the phone with the client, usually with the CFO or Senior Vice President of Strategy. You help qualm any concerns they may have about the status of the deal and update them on where the work stands. They will in turn update their CEO. You call the Vice President or Managing Director on the deal immediately after the call to update them on your conversation with the client. They are grateful for how you handled any issues and direct you on how to proceed next.

10:00 a.m.: You check in with the various analysts on your deal teams to answer any of their questions and make sure they are managing the right priorities for the day. The worst thing would be to find out late in the afternoon that they completed an entire analysis incorrectly, or that they didn't do it at all because directions were unclear. Getting in the habit of checking in regularly can pay off big dividends for all individuals involved.

11:00 a.m.: You get on a call between your client and a potential company they're acquiring. Your job is mostly to mediate and make sure that you are getting questions answered. Occasionally, you interrupt to clarify something or ask a follow-up question. The responses will be important in helping you value and determine the bid for this target company.

You also want to make sure that the two parties maintain a good relationship and that no one side says something inappropriate to the other. For some, this may be their first banking deal, and nerves are running high because it means a big change for the company. Your job is to guide all participants through the process, even though many might be much older and more experienced in life than you! This is why maturity and finesse are so important to being a good associate.

12:00 p.m.: Grab a quick lunch with fellow associates, analysts, or a Vice President.

1:00 p.m.: Get ready for your afternoon meeting with a client. The senior team members will depend on you to answer any questions about the analysis, so it's important that you know it in and out. It was the analyst who did it but it will be your reputation on the line if there are any mistakes! Being skilled at checking someone else's work will become your greatest skill. You will learn to take out your calculator and check numbers by hand.

2:00 p.m.: You check in with the analyst on another deal before running off to your client meeting. Thankfully, the analyst on your project arrived at the conference room early, as instructed, and made sure that the projector was working properly (technical issues make everyone look bad!).

Your assistant escorts the client to the room and you get ready to begin. After the Managing Director has opened the meeting and discussed strategic considerations, you begin to present your latest findings on the analysis. You answer any questions and feel relieved that your part is largely over.

3:30 p.m.: You instruct the analyst on what needs to get done for the remainder of the day and get back to your desk to answer emails you missed during your meeting.

5:00 p.m.: You begin reviewing a model that was sent to you by another group or a client. It takes you some time to figure out how it works, but you eventually have a good grasp of its structure. You decide how to incorporate it into your existing analysis and contact the analyst to schedule a time to sit down and explain your rationale.

The role of an analyst is to create and maintain the model, but the role of an associate is to make sure the model is correct and to provide the assumptions that drive it.

7:30 p.m.: You order dinner with colleagues from Seamless.com. Or, if you're able to, you make plans to eat out with friends or your significant other. You spend the next hour praying that you won't have to break those plans and disappoint your loved ones!

8:00 p.m.: A more senior team member drops by your desk on their way home to recap on the day's outcome. They thank you for how you handled the client meeting and how great the analysis was, and tell you this deal is definitely going to happen and it's going to be big!

You get excited that all the hard work you've put in is being noticed and stop by the analyst's desk to fill them in on the good feedback you've both just received. Fortunately, the senior member also stopped by their desk to thank them, so they're already as excited as you are.

9:00 p.m.: You review a set of slides or a memorandum you just received from an analyst. You take out one of your many handy red pens and start marking up the document. You fix things that the analyst might not have caught, like changing the title of the slide now that the content has drastically changed, or updating a chart given that the underlying numbers are now different. You hand back the red-lined slides to the analyst, make sure that there are no questions, and get ready to head home.

10:30 p.m.: You call it a night and go home. You might hit print on the latest deck of slides to bring home with you in case the Managing Director emails or phones with questions later that night or the next morning. You always have to be prepared to answer questions, since they will likely reach out to you before reaching out to an analyst.

The job of an associate is to essentially serve as the glue of a deal team, managing both up and down the hierarchy as well as managing sideways (client, lawyers, accountants, buyers, other groups, etc.). This is why an associate spends most of the day on calls and meetings while checking the work of an analyst in between and providing the right direction.

11:00 p.m.: You get home and consider whether you should meet your friends at the lounge for a few drinks, or whether they are going to be trouble and you'd better stay in. Your other half is excited you got home "early" and forces you out for a night on the town. You head out, Blackberry in hand, "just in case . . ."

XIV.

How To Succeed At Your Investment Banking Job

"The benefits of working remarkably hard at the beginning, seeking and listening to feedback, and getting involved in extracurriculars can significantly improve the future lifestyle of a banking professional."

First-Year Pointers

After all the hard work to get into banking, now you can start the really hard work of succeeding at your investment banking job. During your career, you will become your own personal cheerleader, helping you get through the long days and early mornings. You can also become the one that will cut corners and sabotage your chances of steadily rising up the ladder of success. Never forget that working hard in your first year is the key to future promotion. Consistently ask for feedback to help you understand what other things you should be doing or how you can improve your performance. Get involved, show team spirit, and go the extra mile to set yourself apart from the pack

Now, after all that, you have been offered a sign-on bonus and a full-time job with the bank you really wanted to join. The culture is a great fit, and the group or product is exactly what you wanted. You're ecstatic. You walk around campus like you're floating on a cloud and you can't stop smiling. At last, you've arrived. Once the buzz wears off and you've been in your job for a few months, you realize your experience can steadily improve if you put in the work or can steadily deteriorate if you don't pay attention.

Following these three simple tips will help take you from a strong performer to a star performer. In return, you will be compensated at the top of the bonus pool. (However, the non-monetary compensation will far outweigh the increase in your bonus!)

1. **Rookie**.

The first year is the most important year, and working hard is the key to future promotion. During this time, just put your head down and work. The banking industry is entirely based on reputation, and you need to build yours. If you do a good job, everyone will know it. If you do a poor job, everyone will know it.

Your first six months after signing on should be spent working extremely hard and always being accessible to your deal teams—even on weekends, holidays, and your birthday. If you're an associate, you may have to do a lot of analyst work to get up to speed. That's okay, this will build the right foundation. If you prove yourself during this initial period, you could reap the benefits for many years to come.

2. **How Am I Doing?**

You should also take the opportunity during this time to consistently ask for feedback. This will help you avoid building bad habits and ensure that your reputation remains untarnished.

Think of it like your college GPA: you start with a 4.0, and it's up to you to maintain it with every class. If you waited until your last class in your senior year to check your GPA, it would be too late to do anything about it—that's why you check on the progress of your GPA every semester. The same goes for your performance in banking. You only get one chance to make a good impression on senior team members, so it's important that you always put your best foot forward.

3. **Good, Great, Excellent**.

What can really set you apart from all the other first-year investment bankers is to go for extra credit. There is no easier way to build your reputation as a strong contributor than to get involved in group committees or firm-wide initiatives.These are also a fun way to get your mind off work!

Participation in these types of non-work activities—like recruiting, training, or planning social events—gives you exposure to people throughout the bank, including senior management. It also shows that you can do more than just excel on your deals. Everyone always waits for the second year to get involved once they're more settled, but that's precisely when it becomes less impressive and more expected. This type of involvement is expected of senior partners, so it's impressive when junior team members display the same quality early on in their careers. Starting early will teach you to manage your time wisely, and will allow you to begin building relationships with senior individuals throughout the bank from day one. That type of exposure is priceless and you will rarely get it through your deals in your first year.

Once you've proven yourself to be a hard worker who is dependable, engaged, and proactive, you will have gained the respect of your staff and superiors. They will give you freedom to choose certain projects and will let you manage some of your time as you see fit. If you promise to get something done by a certain date, your superiors will believe you and will avoid micro-managing the entire process. This means that if you decide to attend your friend's birthday tonight and finish working on the deliverable tomorrow, they won't interfere in your plans. They trust that what you put on their desk tomorrow will be a high-quality work product that will require minimal revisions.

Bottom line: The benefits of working remarkably hard at the beginning, seeking and listening to feedback, and getting involved in extracurriculars can significantly improve the future lifestyle of a banking professional.

XV

Conclusion

". . . you should find it fortunate that the road to becoming a banker may be difficult, but it is far from long, and the steps to getting there are clearly defined. If you work hard and follow the advice outlined in this book, I have no doubt that you can arrive."

Closing Thoughts

Your mind is spinning. You've read about the long hours, the competitive recruiting process, and you're wondering if you can handle the challenges of applying to investment banking, or if you even want to become a banker at all! In closing, I would like to leave you with a few words of wisdom, to help make sense of any lingering confusing thoughts.

It has been my pleasure to be a part of helping you achieve your career vision. Although there were many late nights and canceled plans during my time in banking, I enjoyed the experience tremendously and found it exceptionally rewarding. It is one of the defining chapters in my life. Much of its success came from choosing the right firm, having a supportive family, and turning work colleagues into lifelong friends and mentors. I hope you will someday be able to say the same about your experience in investment banking.

The Value of a Trial Period

Choosing the right career path is a decision that you should not take lightly. For most people, it is the beginning of a lifelong commitment to whatever field they enter. Once you begin on a path, it becomes difficult to completely switch directions without having to start from scratch, take a pay cut, or lose the headway you worked so hard to attain. This does not make it impossible by any means; it simply makes it challenging and best avoided.

For these reasons, **it is crucial to investigate whether banking is right for you before you dive in head first**. There is a good reason why banks mainly hire from their classes of interns: these individuals have already tried the product and liked it! What better assurance for an employer that the new hires will be committed to their jobs? This is especially true for associates, since analysts can choose to go back to graduate school and essentially reset their careers.

An internship is not only one of the only ways to get a full-time position these days, but it is also the only way for you to be sure that you are committing to the right job. I can't stress enough how valuable it can be to your career, and ultimately to your well-being.

A Steep Road Leads to Rewarding Careers

Like any other job that offers a lot of responsibility, a life-changing learning experience, and attractive compensation, the road to get there is not expected to be easy. Think of the many years and hard work students invest to become lawyers, doctors, or professors.

Pursuing a profession in investment banking is no different, but that means it's probably worth it! Don't let the simple reality of a challenging path discourage you. Instead, you should find it fortunate that the road to becoming a banker may be difficult, but it is far from long, and the steps to getting there are clearly defined. If you work hard and follow the advice outlined in this book, I have no doubt that you can arrive.

Training in Banking Opens Doors

I like to think of banking as a type of boot camp. It is intense, not intended for the faint-hearted, and can be transformational. The discipline and critical thinking you learn, both professionally and personally, can be applied towards problem-solving of any nature in the for-profit or non-profit arenas. Some will choose to stay past the boot camp and become a "lifer," a banker who stays on for life. Most will take the training they learn and put it towards a different endeavor, in finance or in another field.

My former colleagues have pursued all sorts of careers after banking, from conventional ones like working at a hedge fund or private equity firm, to more unconventional ones like alleviating poverty through microfinance or starting their own businesses.

As a banker, the service that you render will involve advising companies on how to sustain and grow their businesses, and helping them execute once they have set their visions. The forward-looking and execution skills you gain from providing this type of service will prepare you to pursue any future goals you may set for yourself.

Don't Forget Who You Are

The night before my superday, when I was a 20 year-old student in college, my older brother Richard sent me a long email. I had to wake up early to catch a flight to New York and couldn't help feeling excruciatingly nervous about the events of the following day. I had worked so hard over the last few months to prepare for these interviews.

In his email, Richard tried to put things in perspective for me. He reminded me of who I had been as a little girl growing up in Montreal, Canada, after escaping war in Lebanon. As someone who knew my entire life history, he asked me to remember all the challenges I had faced in life up until that point, and listed specific examples that reconnected me with my inner self. He instructed me to walk into those interviews with the confidence that I could get the job done and show the recruiters who I really was.

It was the best advice anyone had given me: "remember who you are." I have since shared this advice with every person I have coached on job or school applications. If you have done your best to be prepared and can show the evaluators all of who you are, then you can trust that the outcome will be in your best interest. You don't want to look back at the recruiting process and feel that recruiters didn't get to hear about a quality or experience that defined you. Recruiters will not hire someone who they think will be miserable as a banker, whether it's because of a misfit with the job or a cultural misfit with the firm. You don't want to work at a place either where you will be unhappy. Give a well-rounded impression of who you are through your application and you will be victorious no matter what the outcome. Be honest, sincere, and don't forget who you are . . .

Bonus: Resume Template

Use the below links to download your investment banking resume template!

For PDF: http://dl.dropbox.com/u/15229468/Resume%20Template%20V2.pdf

For Microsoft Word
(.docx): http://dl.dropbox.com/u/15229468/Resume%20Template%20V2.docx

Thanks!

Donna

RESUME TEMPLATE

Name

Mailing address
City, State Zip code
Professional E-mail Address ←[no nicknames or numbers]
Phone number

Education

Dates   **SCHOOL NAME**   **City, State (XX) or Country if abroad**

Degree in Major, Concentration/Minors if applicable; GPA
Honors: [List all honors, awards, victories, and scholarships]
Activities: [List all extracurricular activities including any leadership positions; ideally this should show that you are well-rounded, so a strong mix would have some sports, community service, industry club, and other unique activities dealing perhaps with student government, cultural awareness, the arts, etc. Use verbs such as "elected", "founded", or "selected" when appropriate to highlight the process you underwent to become a leader or a member.]

Experience

Dates   **COMPANY NAME**   **City, State (XX) or Country if abroad**
            Title

[Description of company if it is not a well-known firm. Otherwise, you can choose to include a statement that summarizes the position, but this is not required.]

- Most important achievement ← [Make sure to be very specific in stating exactly what you did, with whom, and what contribution it made; if appropriate, try to convey any challenges and how you overcame them; quantify the impact or result of your work with a numerical estimate if possible (e.g. dollars sold, number of new customers).]
- Another achievement ← [Make sure that you are not simply repeating the same point as above in different words; each achievement should convey something new about your responsibilities and skills; use specific action verbs like "Lead", "Motivated", "Analyzed", "Supervised", "Executed", "Launched", etc., rather than the same generic verbs.]
- Least important achievement ← [Your hope is that the recruiter will read all of these bullets, but make sure that the first ones are the most impressive in case they don't make it further down the list! Remember to mention any contributions that are not directly related to your role like involvement in training, recruiting, or firm-wide initiatives.]
- [If you have too many bullets or held two roles in one position, you can organize them by business function (e.g. Marketing, Product Development, Operations) or by task (e.g. Project Management, Analytics).]
- [If you worked on transactions or public projects, you can include a section titled "Selected Transaction Experience" and list them; include name of companies involved, type of transaction, and deal size if appropriate.]

Skills   [This last section should add some personality to your resume and ensure that a recruiter has a good sense of who you are; ask yourself "what attributes about me are missing from my resume?"; you can list languages, technical expertise, certifications (CPA, CFA, FINRA, etc.), publications, patents, business ventures you founded, or non-profit work; note that it's no longer necessary to list skills like "Microsoft Word" on your resume, so skip it!]

Interests   [One line listing 3-5 of your hobbies; don't just say "art", specify the kind of art. This was my favorite section to read as a recruiter, so don't ignore it! Be aware that anything you list may become a topic in your interview...]

meeting and realized that I had been leading the entire session with black raccoon eyes, remnants of the safety goggles and rubber residue…!

What is your favorite quote and why?

I love many quotes, but one that I live by is: "There are those who make money, and those who make history." It was engrained in me by my father who is an artist. I love how it pushes you to think beyond society's definitions of success.

What did you want to be when you were growing up?

I always wanted to be an actress. In sixth grade, I was elected President of my elementary school (after much campaigning during recess!). Kids from younger grades would stop me in the hallway and ask for my "autograph", and I always used to say, "Hold on to this! It will be worth a lot of money someday when I became an actress…" I now live in Hollywood, so it's not over yet!

About the Publisher

Hyperink is the easiest way for anyone to publish a beautiful, high-quality book.

We work closely with subject matter experts to create each book. We cover topics ranging from higher education to job recruiting, from Android apps marketing to barefoot running.

If you have interesting knowledge that people are willing to pay for, especially if you've already produced content on the topic, please reach out to us! There's no writing required and it's a unique opportunity to build your own brand and earn royalties.

Hyperink is based in SF and actively hiring people who want to shape publishing's future. Email us if you'd like to meet our team!

Note: If you're reading this book in print or on a device that's not web-enabled, **please email** books@hyperinkpress.com with the title of this book in the subject line. We'll send you a PDF copy, so you can access all of the great content we've included as clickable links.

Get in touch:

Made in the USA
Middletown, DE
22 May 2017